Captain Cook Explores the South Seas

CAPTAIN COOK

EXPLORES

THE SOUTH SEAS

Written and Illustrated by

ARMSTRONG SPERRY

RANDOM HOUSE · NEW YORK

Second Printing

Copyright 1955 by Armstrong Sperry
All rights reserved under International and
Pan-American Copyright Conventions
Published in New York by Random House, Inc.
and simultaneously in Toronto, Canada by
Random House of Canada Ltd.
Library of Congress Catalog Card Number: 55-5827
Manufactured in the United States of America.

Contents

Captain Cook Explores
the South Seas

1 The Song of the Sea

That August morning in the year 1741, the early sun was as bright as a promise of good fortune. It cast a light of gold over the rolling moors of Yorkshire, on fat sheep grazing in the fields. It lay warm as a blessing on the shoulders of the boy who followed so eagerly an empty road that stretched forever away from Great Ayton.

Mark that boy well, Reader! For young James Cook—tall for his thirteen summers, and with all his belongings swinging in a bundle at the end of a stick—had set forth on a great adventure. Although in years to come he was to travel farther over the earth's surface than any man before him, perhaps this first youthful journey was the most momentous of all. It set the pattern of his future.

The fishing village called Staithes, whither he was bound, lay a full day's walk from Great Ayton. Already the boy had covered ten miles, but he would have to hurry to reach his destination before nightfall. In Staithes, James Cook was to serve for a term of three years as apprentice to one William Saunderson, grocer.

"A *grocer!*" James's father had scoffed. "To stand all day behind a counter, selling bags of sugar and sacks of flour! What sort of a life is that for a lad who can plow a straight furrow and bind wheat with the best? Answer me that, eh?"

"But Staithes, Dadder, is at the sea's edge!" the boy had cried. "I have never seen the sea, or a ship."

"No more have I." The man thrust out his

Young James Cook was setting out on a great adventure

chin stubbornly. "All this blather about ships! The plow is good enough for me. Why not for you? Your brothers are content to stay at home and help me in the fields."

The brothers had glanced at James uncertainly, as a flock of chicks might eye the only duckling in their midst as it took to water. The oldest one demanded, "And what do you think to learn of ships behind a grocer's counter?"

"I'll be within stone's throw of them!" the boy answered. "Oh, I'll learn, never fear."

His mother glanced quickly around the circle. "Leave the lad be, all of you," she protested. "Maybe he comes by it natural. Who can say?"

Yes, perhaps that was the root of the matter. On one side of her family, Grace Cook's people (unlike those of her farmer husband) had been seafarers. Often on winter evenings the woman had filled the ears of her young son with half-remembered tales of far lands that lay beyond the vast rolling ocean. She spoke of Spaniards and Norsemen and many others, even of those who belonged to no nation and of whom one spoke in whispers—pirates! In his mind's eye young James could see them all. And although he had never actually heard it, the sea already had begun to sing its everlasting song in his ear, just as it hummed within the white conch shell that lay on the mantel above the fireplace. Uncle Gwillim had brought that shell all the way from Africa.

"Hold it once to yer ear and listen, lad," his

uncle had warned, "and ye'll never be content on the land again. I tell ye, the sea's a wild and wonderful music in a man's blood. But she's a cruel mistress, laddie. Never listen to her song unless ye be willing to die with the sound of it in yer ears."

James listened. Perhaps his mother was right and he "came by it natural." He knew only that he wanted to live with the song of the sea forever.

Though his father had grumbled and protested, the man felt in his bones that this son of his, so set apart from the others, would never be content to plow the soil. The salt sea was in the boy's blood, just as the blue of it was in his eyes. Reluctantly the man had scratched his name on the papers that would apprentice young James to William Saunderson, grocer.

Between hedgerows of hawthorn the empty road stretched toward a future that was free and fine and unknown. The only certainty was that at the end of the road James Cook would find the sea. The boy's stride lengthened, leaving the miles behind.

Already his square-toed boots with the pewter buckles and his coarse stockings were powdered with dust. Sweat dampened his shirt. He gave a hitch to the belt of his homespun breeches and settled the staff more comfortably on his shoulder. He broke into a high-pitched whistle while a bird in the hedgerow cocked its head to listen. But although the boy looked so eagerly ahead, the thought of all that he was leaving behind passed like a sudden cloud-shadow across his mind. He saw the snug stone cottage in Marton, where he had been born in October of 1728, and the fields of Great Ayton (a neighboring hamlet) where he had toiled at his father's side. He recalled the elderly spinster, Dame Walker, the schoolmistress of the village. It was she who had taught him to read, paying special attention to geography and mathematics —the two subjects in which young James seemed to have particular skill. And then his heart thumped for a moment as he thought of his brothers crowding round him that morning to say good-bye; the mute, awkward grip of his father's worn hand; the flash of his mother's tenderness, like a rainbow, as she clung to him to whisper, "God keep you, son, and bring you home." When would he see them all again and hear their voices? The brave whistle died in the boy's throat. He swallowed hard.

But on such a day, on such a journey, it was impossible to be downcast for long. Clouds raced across the English sky, like white-sailed ships tacking before the wind. Now and again farmers working in their fields paused to call a greeting. Dogs barked a warning. Children stared, silent and wide-eyed. The boy took a packet of bread and cheese from his pocket and wolfed it down. He paused beside a brook only long enough to quench his thirst. What would William Saunderson, his future employer, be like? James's father had heard about the man by chance, but no one in Great Ayton knew him. Three years was a long time in which to serve any but a kind master! Would it be so terrible to stand behind a counter and sell flour, as his father insisted? James could find no answer to these uncertainties as he watched the shadows lengthen with the passing hours.

The character of the lonely moorland began to change, giving way at last to rockier, sterner ground. Villages were few. Trees grew sparser and their limbs pointed inland, as if driven by an unseen wind. As the sun dipped into the west, fatigue for the first time pulled at the boy's muscles. But he only quickened his step. Long hours of working in the fields, under the hot suns of summer, had toughened his wiry body. Hunger, however, was another matter. It seemed hours since he had eaten the bread and cheese! Surely, James thought, his new employer would see to it that he didn't go to bed on an empty stomach.

The wind freshened and the boy sniffed at it eagerly, for his mother had told him that salt air could be smelled from miles away. Yes, there was no doubt about it! There *was* a different tang to the air already! It held no familiar, drowsy scent of loam or hay. It was clean and cool and alive. It set the blood tingling in his veins.

Suddenly a dull and distant rumbling came to James's ear. A thunderstorm in the making, perhaps. . . . But the late-afternoon sky, serene and untroubled, held no hint of storm. The booming sound of thunder increased, stirring in the hair on the boy's scalp. And then James Cook understood. What he heard was not thunder. It was the living voice of the sea!

A cry broke from his lips. His pace quickened to a half-run as he climbed the last steep hill that lay before him. At its crest he drew up short. A salt wind greeted him with a rush and a roar. Below, diminished by distance, the village of Staithes lay cradled in a cleft of barren hills. A single cobbled street curved along the bay, bordered by stone cottages that stood elbow to elbow; and there were wharves where fishermen landed their scaly cargoes and hung their nets to dry.

But it was the sea that claimed and transfixed the boy's attention. To the north, as far as the eye could reach, it glittered in the dying light, filling his soul with wonder. Surf pounded against the rocks and dissolved in spray, while gray-backed gulls screeched as they soared on rigid wings along the currents of the air. James Cook stood stock-still. He felt as if all the sinews of his body had been plucked by an unseen hand and set a-humming, as a vessel's cordage hums to a sudden-bursting gale. He wanted to shout and sing, but his tongue was silent. It was all strange, yet he felt that he had known it always.

In the harbor a fleet of fishing boats was snugging down for the night. Here and there lights began to gleam. The first star appeared, flickering with pallid fire. A rough, wheel-furrowed road twisted down across the hill toward Staithes, still a good two miles distant. The boy drew a deep breath. Then, squaring his shoulders, he followed where the road led.

Thus James Cook—who until that day had never been farther than five miles from his own hearthside—came at last to the sea.

2   The Young Apprentice

By the time the boy reached the outskirts of Staithes, darkness had fallen. The cobbled street leading into the town was empty. There was no sound except the surf's muted thunder as it rode the back of the night wind. The shutters of the cottage windows were closed, lending the place a dark, unfriendly aspect. The boy drew up uncertainly. Which way should he turn?

At that moment a seagoing figure rounded the

corner—a sailor who pulled up short to avoid meeting James in head-on collision.

"Avast there, me bucko!" the man cried. "Don't you know 'tis time to make home port for the night?"

"I'm sorry, sir," the boy stammered. "But I'm a stranger to this port."

"Stranger, eh? And whose house might ye be seekin'?"

"That of William Saunderson, grocer."

The sailor's jaw dropped. He bent a curious eye on the boy, then said, "Bear straight ahead for a furlong, bub. Then larboard yer helm and ye'll see a sign hangin' hand-spike high. That'll be the shop of William Saunderson."

"My thanks to you, sir."

"No thanks due, matey," came the answer. "But tell me—what business might a country-feed lad like yourself be havin' with such a man as that one?"

"What do you mean, sir?" the boy faltered.

"Stop callin' me 'sir,' like I was a ruddy King's officer," the other retorted. "As for that William Saunderson—you should be told that he's a sharp one. 'Tis common knowledge he'd skin a flea for the hide and tallow."

James swallowed. "But I am apprenticed to him—for a term of three years."

The sailor gave a low whistle. "Weary winds! *Another* apprentice, eh? Ah, well, 'tis none o' my affair. Just keep a weather eye to wind'ard, matey. Ye're a rugged-lookin' lad, and William Saunderson's but a wee squirt of a man. I'll wager a pound sterling to a plug o' Irish twist that you can fend for yourself. May God be your guiding!"

Whereupon the stranger swung away with his rolling gait, leaving behind a forlorn boy who suddenly felt anything but resourceful. Behind what the sailor actually had said, there had sounded a note of warning. Why, James wondered, might he be called upon to fend for himself? What manner of man would "skin a flea for the hide and tallow"? And what had the sailor meant by saying *"another* apprentice"? As the boy pursued his way, his legs felt curiously weighted and home seemed far, far off. But before he had gone many paces, he discovered a sign swinging in the wind and heard the complaint of its rusty irons. He read the fateful words: WILLIAM SAUNDERSON, *Grocer.*

Before long he discovered a sign swinging in the wind

The house itself was built of dark stone. Anxiously the boy scanned it for some sign of life. No smoke issued from the chimney pots, and one black window still unshuttered gaped like a sightless eye. The heavy door had a bleak, forbidding look. For a second the boy felt a blind impulse to bolt and run. Then his chin came up in sudden determination. He gripped the iron knocker and let it fall. The noise was appalling. Utter silence followed. Above that silence James could hear the dull pounding of his heart.

An upper window flung open. A head, crowned with a knitted cap, thrust forth; but darkness blurred the shape of the man's features. "Who stands there and what seek ye?" came a rasping voice.

"Sir—" James began.

" 'Tis no hour to sound the knocker," the other interrupted. "This shop is closed for the night."

The boy tried again. "But, I—"

"Be off with you!" the man shouted. "If your mother forgot to buy a bag of salt, 'tis no fault of mine. Return at a decent hour in the morning."

"But I haven't come to buy salt—" The boy's voice was rising with resentment.

"Then if ye're here as a beggar, get you gone—before I lay a cane across your backside!"

A heat of anger swept James Cook. No one had ever spoken to him in such a tone. He squared his shoulders and flung up his chin in the gesture with which, all his life, he was to meet a crisis. "My name is James Cook," he called back loudly. "I am your apprentice. I must say I expected a more civil greeting!"

By this frontal attack William Saunderson was momentarily silenced. Then he rallied and snapped, "My new apprentice, eh? It has taken you long enough to get here—with an impudent tongue to boot. Stand where you be till I unlock the door."

Still fuming at such a reception, young James stood his ground. Presently he heard a patter of footsteps, quick and light. Then came the clank of a chain as the bolt shot back. The door slid open.

"Come in, come in!" The querulous voice seemed to issue from nowhere. "Don't stand there like a dolt. The wind has strong teeth and there's little enough fuel in the house."

Gingerly James crossed the threshold. At once the heavy door slammed shut behind him. The bolt slipped quickly into place. The boy came about to face his future employer—and a stranger figure he had never imagined. William Saunderson was a small-boned man, nimble as a fox. Under the knitted cap his sharp-pointed features and bristling whiskers lent him an aspect which, also, was singularly foxlike. By the light of the candle which he held in one hand, his eyes were close-set and of surpassing brightness, like highly polished green stones. The other hand clutched a cane as if it were a bludgeon. Though the man was, in truth, half a head shorter than the boy who confronted him, there was something about the foxy eyes, the clawlike hands, that seemed infinitely dangerous. And instinctively James Cook clenched his fists, as if to meet an actual threat. Under the piercing scrutiny of the man's green eyes he flushed with resentment.

"H'mmm . . ." muttered William Saunderson, as if he didn't like what he saw. "My new apprentice, eh? Ye'll step smart when I speak, boy, or ye'll feel the weight of this cane."

James got himself in hand, although he was

seething with anger. It would never do to antagonize his employer at the very outset of his service.

"I have a letter for you, sir," he managed. "My father bade me give it you at once."

"Hand it here!"

Nimble fingers twitched the folded sheet of paper from the boy's hand. The man lifted the candle high, and with the movement black shadows leaped along the wall. Half aloud William Saunderson began to read the words that James's father had so laboriously inscribed.

> *Respected sir:*
>
> The bearer of this letter is my son James, a well-lessoned and industrious boy. He bears likewise my written consent to three years in your service. I charge you to see to his welfare, and to remember that his Sundays belong to the church. In return, James will give you faithful service.
>
> I remain, respected sir,
>
> *James Cook, Senior.*

William Saunderson crumpled the letter and flung it from him. "I trust your father's confidence in you is not misplaced, my fine lad," he said, and quoted with sarcasm, " 'Well-lessoned and industrious.' Ha! We shall see."

"I will do my best, sir—" James brought out.

"That's as may be," the other retorted rudely. "Come, I will show you where you sleep."

The man turned toward a narrow stair that led upward into darkness. James's heart sank with the certainty that there would be no supper, but he followed dutifully at his employer's heels. Silhouetted against the glow of the candle, William Saunderson looked like a monstrous spider climbing the web of the stairs. And the boy felt as helpless as a fly blundering into that web. For a second he was seized with panic. His heart beat like the wings of a pigeon in a trap.

At the top of the stairs stood a closed door. The man drew back a bolt. He thrust the candle into James's hand.

"Your bed is in the garret," he snapped. "You will rise at five sharp, set the porridge to boil, and sweep out the shop. You hear me, boy?"

"Yes—sir," James managed.

The man shook his cane. "Remember, I'll put

up with no slugabeds. You're here to work and
work ye shall!"

Slowly James mounted another steep stair.
At its summit the beams of the garret arched
close above his head. There was a single window
with small round panes, across which generations of spiders had spun their webs. Rats
scurried for cover. From somewhere came the
squeak of a bat. On the floor lay a mattress
stuffed with straw—a wretched-looking pallet,
in all truth, even to a boy so weary and foot-
sore. James removed his boots, loosened his
belt. He took the nightshirt from his bundle,
slipped into it, shivered at its clammy touch.
At home, now, his father would be reading
aloud a page from the Bible, while his mother
washed the supper dishes and put away the left-
over food. . . . Resolutely the boy forced his
thoughts into safer channels. He sank his teeth
into his lower lip to stop its trembling. And
then he knelt beside the mattress, bowed his
head and prayed to God with all his might—
just as he had been taught to do at home.

"Oh, God, in Thy mercy and goodness, please
to humble my stubborn spirit. Please to help

me do my chores right. Bless those who love me and—and soften the hearts of my enemies. For Thy sake, amen!"

From outside came the restless lap of waves against the wharves, while the wind rolled in thundering echoes along the shore. The boy blew out the candle. Then, heavy in spirit and empty of stomach, he lay down to a fitful, tossing sleep.

When, in after years, James Cook grew up and thought at all about his childhood, this scene always remained, over and beyond the others. He wondered sometimes why it was that he remembered it so clearly when more recent events often were clouded. Then he understood: it was because on the night that found him in the dark and lonely garret of William Saunderson, the door of childhood closed behind him forever. Ahead stretched the long, uncertain road down which he must go as a man.

During the weeks and months that followed, young James Cook was to learn that the lot of an apprentice, under such a master as William Saunderson, was not rosy. By five in the morning the hammering of a cane would sound on the garret door, accompanied by the cry, "Up, ye lazy numbskull! Up, I say!"

Sweeping and cleaning the shop. Scrubbing down the stairs. Breakfast at seven—seldom more than a slice of bread covered with molasses, or a bowl of thin porridge. Throughout the long hours of the day the boy was on his feet serving customers—measuring sugar and flour, weighing cheese and salt herring, running senseless errands. But though he strove to fulfill his many duties to the best of his ability, James quickly discovered that there was no pleasing his employer. Nothing he did ever seemed right. Often the cane descended on his shoulders with stinging blows.

William Saunderson would frequently remark, "A boy who steals time for which he is paid is as much a thief as one who steals a farthing from his master's pocket."

And the man saw to it that his young apprentice found few hours that could be stolen, even had James been so inclined. Only on Sundays did the boy enjoy a brief respite. Then, returning from church, he never failed to seek the company of the fishermen who knew no day of rest. They soon came to accept as one of themselves the thin lad, so steady-eyed and self-reliant, so eager to hear their yarns about the deep sea. It was the memory of those salty tales that carried the boy through the tasks and humiliations of the week. Often he worked as in a trance, in imagination seeing the blood-red suns of Africa, the palm trees of the Indies that were said to be as green as the heart of an emerald. And always within sight and sound there was the sea. . . . More and more James came to inhabit a dream world that was vastly more real to him than the grim world of his apprentice-ship, or than the blows of his employer. Even in sleep his dreams were colored by visions of great uncharted continents, of coral islands still to be discovered, drowsing in a sunlit sea. . . .

One fine September morning, more than a year after James Cook had sounded the knocker on the front door, the porridge went uncooked, the shop unswept.

William Saunderson was in a towering rage. He hammered against the garret door. "Come down here, ye idle sculp!" he thundered. "Oh,

but ye shall have the cane for this! Come down,
I say!"

There was no answer. James Cook, like all
the other apprentices who had served this same
tyrannical master, had run away.

3 The Turning Point

Some nine miles south of Staithes, under lofty cliffs, the ancient port of Whitby lay on the banks of the river Esk. The Britons, the Romans, the Saxons, the Danes and the Normans— all had left their imprint on this sheltered corner of the Yorkshire coast. The abbey of St. Hilda dominated the town, and in its shadow

the red brick houses of the shipowners and merchants climbed the narrow streets.

That year of 1746 found Whitby a thriving
seaport. Here ships were being built and rigged.
Here they set forth on voyages to the ends of
the known world. Here they returned, heavy
with ivory and spices and whalebone. And here
finally they rode at anchor, the rake of their
masts beckoning like a finger to any lad who
stood on the threshold of adventure.

One such was young James Cook. That morning before daybreak he had crossed the high
meadows and skirted the moors that left Staithes
(and William Saunderson) behind him. Never
again would he jump to obey the sound of any
man's voice, or submit to the humiliation of
being beaten. For better or worse he was his
own master now. There was no turning back.

Even as the boy hesitated, wondering what his
next move should be, he was caught up by the
humming industry of the water front. From every cooperage came the clatter of maul against
hoop and stave; from every smithy the clang of
sledge on red-hot iron; from every ropewalk the
hum of hemp fiber spinning into stout line. Oh,

but this was vastly more exciting than a peaceful fishing village like Staithes! James gave a hitch to his belt and strode confidently into the town.

Not far ahead, built out on a stone wharf, stood a brick building with a sign that proclaimed:

MESSRS. JOHN & HENRY WALKER
Merchants

Beside the wharf a square-rigged ship lay moored, across whose stern the name was lettered in gilt: *Freelove*. Though grimed and sooty with the cargoes of coal that she carried in the North Sea trade, the hull of the *Freelove* was as clean-lined as a greyhound—all pride and beauty and strength. From her bowsprit sprang the carved figure of an angel with trumpet poised, like a herald of good tidings. And James's heart danced within him. In that moment he could not have guessed the part this vessel was to play in his future; he knew only that the *Freelove* was such a ship as he had dreamed one day of finding. Boldly he knocked

at the door of the Messrs. Walker's establish-
ment and entered.

A man with sandy hair glanced up from a
table that was littered with charts and nautical
paraphernalia. Behind square-cut, steel-rimmed
spectacles a pair of blue eyes twinkled with good
nature—shrewd eyes, none the less, that ap-
praised the boy's sturdy frame, his straight and
level Yorkshire gaze.

"What might the nature of your errand be,
young fellow-my-lad?" came the mild query.

At the friendliness of the man's tone, James
took heart. He had been so long accustomed to
his former employer's abuse that he had almost
forgotten there were men of good will in the
world.

"I—I would like to sign as apprentice, sir,"
he brought out.

"Indeed?" the other replied. "And where
might you be from? By your accent, it's certain
you're not of Whitby."

James hesitated. "I come from Great Ayton,
sir."

John Walker's eyes rounded. "A far distance,
in all truth. When did you leave your home—
and *why?*"

The boy drew an uncertain breath. It seemed that everything depended on his answer and on this man's understanding. Then the words came with a rush. "I left home a year and more ago, sir," he blurted. "My father apprenticed me to William Saunderson, in Staithes. But—but I've run away from *him,* sir. I will never go back!"

There followed a moment of silence, during which James could feel his heart thumping at his ribs. Anxiously he scanned the face of the man who eyed him so kindly, yet so shrewdly.

"Saunderson, eh?" John Walker said. "I've never heard good of that man." Then he chuckled. "Ye lasted longer than most of his apprentices, lad. But tell me—do you realize how hard it is—the life aboard a collier? The North Sea can be the wickedest bit o' water in this world. 'Tis no place for a landlubber or a weakling."

"I'm not afraid of hard work," the boy cried, and he flexed his biceps to prove it. "I'm 'most as strong as a man, sir, and willing to learn."

"It will be necessary to have your father's consent," John Walker reminded him.

"I'll dispatch a letter this very day if you say

so," the boy promised eagerly. "Oh, my father will consent, have no doubt."

"So be it," the man answered. "I like the look of you, James Cook. While we're awaiting your father's reply, you may work here in the ship-yard and take lodgings in my own home."

James's spirit bounded upward, as if a great weight had been removed. This man talked to him as a friend, as an equal, offering his home for shelter. The boy's heart swelled with grati-tude.

"You will never have cause to be sorry, sir," he managed. "I will do my best to serve you—"

"I make no doubt of that," John Walker an-swered. " 'Tis not often I mistake the look in a man's eye—or a boy's either. And I'll be bound, ye seem already more man than boy!"

They gripped hands. Walker scribbled a note.

"Carry this paper to my wife," he said. "She'll take ye under her wing and find a room for you, and a meal that will stick to your ribs. God's blessing on you, lad."

Blind chance had led James to the doors of Messrs. John and Henry Walker. He could not have been more fortunate. This was a turning point in his life.

In due time an answer to the boy's letter came from Great Ayton. James Cook, Senior, gave his consent to the new apprenticeship. He spoke of the family's welfare, of the crops and cattle. He admonished his son to be a good boy, to remember his prayers at night and to discharge his duties honorably. He hoped that one day, in God's good time, the family might be reunited under the home roof. . . .

With his father's blessing, and with a few belongings packed in a canvas bag, young James went aboard the *Freelove* at once. He could hardly contain his elation. He was a sailor.

He was going to sea!

In the weeks to come, the boy was to discover that life aboard a North Sea collier (as John Walker had warned) was not easy. The *Freelove* carried a cargo of hard English coal along the stormy coastal waters to Newcastle and London. There were days and nights filled with the misery of seasickness. There was the appalling fear that James had to conquer every time he climbed the swaying masts and lay out on the yardarms to furl sail. There was the bewildering maze of rigging to be learned, the names of sails as foreign to his ear as the sound of a heathen tongue. There were the two-fisted officers putting the fear of God into those who shirked or faltered. And there were James's rough-and-ready shipmates of the fo'c'sle: men hardened in the toughest of schools. Here a boy grew up almost overnight.

Like the greenest hand aboard, young James knew that life in the British merchant service was vastly preferable to that of the Royal Navy; and the Walker ships were superior to most. Their voyages were of short duration and the men were paid wages regularly. But despite these considerations, the North Sea runs were punishment for ships and men alike. Winds were erratic, currents treacherous. Fog, shoals, lee shores were ever-present dangers. Under a poor navigator a ship enjoyed a short life. James came quickly to believe that sailing across the wide ocean would be a simple matter compared to outwitting the perils of offshore navigation.

In the wintry climate of the British Isles the cold penetrated the very marrow of a man's bones. Below decks, in the *Freelove*, the fo'c'sle was ever awash, hammocks were eternally wet, the food was half cooked and unpalatable. Often spars and rigging were caked with ice. Sails, frozen solid, must be hammered into submission by bloody fists. Under such conditions the price of survival was skill. In the hardest possible way young James Cook began to learn the fundamentals of seamanship. What he learned he remembered. Those who forgot paid for the blunder with their life.

Yet never for a moment, even in the darkest hours, did the boy regret his decision. He was as surely born to follow the sea as his father had been born to guide the plow. He rejoiced in his ability to overcome the obstacles which daily confronted him. The old fears were soon forgotten. Seasickness was a thing of the past. Danger became as heady as wine, and each new victory won against the forces of wind and sea filled the boy with a singing wonder.

From the very beginning of the voyage James had begun to keep a log—a record of the day's passage and the ship's response. Nothing escaped his inquisitive eye. The performance of the *Freelove* under each new sail plan; winds; currents; cloud formations; birds and fishes—all found their way to the water-stained pages of his book.

Though he could not realize it at the time, the young apprentice was laying the foundations of a seamanship that later was to recognize few peers.

With genuine regret the boy discovered that, during the worst months of winter, the Walkers recalled the *Freelove* into home port. But if there was disappointment in leaving the sea, even for a short time, the ensuing weeks spent in the Whitby shipyards proved to have their own special reward. The keel had been laid for a new collier of 600 tons. It would be called the *Three Brothers* and James Cook would have a hand in the building. Also, the rigors and hardships of life at sea were temporarily forgotten in the pleasant household of the Walker family.

Mrs. Walker soon became a second mother to the quiet, serious-minded boy. She saw that his meals were nourishing, she mended his worn clothing; and for the first time James realized how lonely he had been. The library shelves were stacked with books dealing with nautical matters, and the boy took to them as a duck to water. At night, after the supper dishes had been cleared away, he spread his books on the dining-room table. There by candlelight he began to study the knotty problems of navigation. Maps enthralled him, but those large areas marked *incognita*—unknown—stirred him to impatience. True, the map-makers were apt to fill in such areas with fanciful drawings of mermaids and dolphins, or with pictures of Aeolus puffing out a mouthful of winds. But there was a challenge in those unknown spaces that fired the boy's imagination and set him wondering. A map-maker for the Royal Navy, Alexander Dalrymple, had openly asserted that there was a great southern continent in the Antarctic containing 50,000,000 people! How, James wondered, could Dalrymple make such a statement when this supposed continent had never been discovered?

Under John Walker's prompting, James's skill in mathematics grew apace. Almost without effort he seemed to understand figures. Trigonometry was much easier than a page of English composition! Hesitant at first, he began to dip into astronomy and soon found himself absorbed by that ancient science. And so while Mrs. Walker saw to the boy's material needs, her husband nourished James's eager mind on the rich fare of the library shelves.

By day, the shipyard offered a never-ending interest. Pile heads had been driven deep into the slip to form a cradle for the growing *Three Brothers*. The air was filled with the tang of fresh-sawed oak and pine. Adze and caulking iron kept up their resounding clamor. Wood powder drifted like mist from the pits where the undersawyers worked, and the fires of the blacksmiths glowed in the wind. But for James Cook the *Three Brothers* was not just one more collier: she was timber and iron springing into life under the workmen's hands. One of his special tasks was helping to plot the intricate web of her rigging. Valuable experience, this. It printed indelibly in the boy's mind the function of every inch of the standing and running rigging of a three-masted ship. More, it convinced him that a North Sea collier was the type of vessel that lay closest to his heart and interest. In this conviction he never wavered.

Thus the seasons, and the years of James's apprenticeship, rolled by. They fled like sea birds in a mist. Months of strenuous voyages at sea alternated with winters spent ashore in the Whitby yards. A boy no longer, but a tall, wide-shouldered young man, James Cook sailed aboard the ships he helped to build; and if there were flaws in hull or mast or rigging, he found the mistakes and corrected them. His knowledge of seamanship grew wide and deep. He came to know the ports of France, of Holland, of Norway and Denmark. The farmer's son from Great Ayton had a firm foot set on the first rung of a high ladder.

But a new spirit was in the air. Europe was seething with intrigue. In Germany, Frederick II of Prussia was athirst for power. Alarmed, France and Russia sided with Austria against him. England's King George II, himself born in Germany, was openly sympathetic to that country. Besides, France and England were tradi-

The ship was coming to life under the workmen's hands

tional enemies, and any move that weakened the former strengthened the latter. Clearly a war of great proportions was simmering. No man could say when it might boil over.

James Cook had heard this talk on the Thames water front, and often he had thrilled to the splendid sight of the King's ships sailing in undisputed mastery of the seas. And suddenly the routine of collier service seemed flat and stale. An idea began to form in his mind. . . .

That afternoon John Walker sent for him. The man seemed to be bursting with news of good import. The grip of his hand was hearty, his smile infectious.

"You sent for me, sir?" James demanded.

"Aye, that I did," the other replied. "From the very beginning you have served my interests unselfishly, James Cook. By your own efforts and perseverance you have gone up and up. You're a true sailor, lad, and I'm proud to shake your hand."

At the hint of surprise in the young man's face, John Walker hurried on. " 'Tis proper time you received the promotion that's your rightful due. I have decided to give you command of the *Friendship*."

The *Friendship* was the newest and finest of the Walker colliers. James's heart leaped. Such an appointment would make him senior officer of the ship he had served on as mate for more than two years. It meant that during the long years he had toiled at sea and in the shipyards, he had mastered his profession, and here was the recognition of it. He looked into the twinkling, honest blue eyes of his old friend and felt a pang at the answer he must give.

"You honor me with such an offer, sir," he said slowly. "I regret more than I can say that I must decline."

"*Decline?*" gasped John Walker, as if he had not heard aright. "Are you daft, son? Here's what you've been working toward all these years."

"I know," the other answered. "But any day now England may find herself at war. I must offer my services to the King."

"But you'd have to start at the very bottom—all over again," John Walker protested. "If war comes, you'll not be pressed into the King's service so long as you've a commission in a merchant ship. Besides, the Royal Navy is snob-ridden. Only gentlemen's sons may become officers."

James Cook gave his slow smile. "And I am only the son of a farmer, without connections or fine friends. But you forget, sir, that unlike many of the gentlemen in the King's service, I *know* ships! I am willing to fight every inch of the way from the fo'c'sle to the quarter-deck. What does it matter if a man be born in a stone cottage or in a castle, so long as he can sail a ship?"

John Walker rose and gripped the young man's hand. A smile of great affection wiped the disappointment from his face. "Your mind's made up, I can see, and there's never been any changing of *that*. Who am I to try? If war does come to this blessed country, it will be men the like of yourself who win it for England. God bless and keep you, James Cook."

The next morning—June 17, 1755—a new able seaman signed aboard His Majesty's ship of war, *Eagle*.

4 A Sailor of the King

Although war had not yet been formally declared, England set up a blockade of the coast
of France. By such means King George hoped
to prevent reinforcements from reaching the
French settlements in Canada, where fighting
between French and English-American colonists
had been going on for over a year. For it was in
the New World that the two nations would come

finally to grips. This was the opinion of William Pitt when he became England's Secretary of State, for he believed that his country's future lay in her wealth of lands abroad. In the name of the Crown, Pitt was to undertake full possession of North America and drive out the French and Spanish for all time. The blockade of France was the opening skirmish.

His Majesty's ship of war *Eagle,* under Captain Joseph Hamer, joined the blockading squadron. James Cook's appointment in the *Eagle* had reduced him to the rank of ordinary seaman. For a man of his humble beginnings, to win recognition in the Royal Navy would be an uphill fight whose outcome could not be predicted. Yet it is characteristic of Cook that, having made a decision, he never cast a backward glance. His blood leaped at the thought of going into action. Already his long apprenticeship in the collier runs of the North Sea seemed dull indeed and far behind. In his heart he knew that a milestone had been passed. The future shone bright with a promise of danger.

Since it was difficult to persuade sailors to enlist in the Royal Navy, men of all sorts were seized and pressed forcibly into service. Many

of them had never been to sea and had no quali-
fications for such a life. The jails were swept
clean of debtors and criminals, who were promised shorter sentences if they joined voluntarily.
Water-front taverns were raided by the King's
men, who dragged their protesting victims willy-
nilly aboard the handiest ship of war.

The crew of the *Eagle* proved to be no excep-
tion. Pickpockets and vagabonds, country louts
and riffraff from the alleys—these were the men
who found their way into the fo'c'sle of the
ship of war. In such sorry company James Cook
loomed like a tower in a fog. Quickly he discovered that in seafaring matters Captain Hamer.
and his officers were barely more competent than
the raw recruits. This was frequently the case
in the Royal Navy, for top-ranking officers were
chosen from the sons of aristocrats who often
could not distinguish between a windlass and a
binnacle. Consequently all King's ships were
provided with a sailing master. It was the duty
of this individual to lay the ship's course, calcu-
late her position at sea and give orders to the
crew for furling and setting sail. Next in line
came the master's mate. These two men were re-
sponsible for sailing the ship. Only during bat-

tle did the officers assume command, and even then only under the watchful eye of the master and the mate.

Captain Hamer soon recognized the superiority of James Cook to his shipmates. Unlike most of that ill-found crew, Cook not only had been to sea, but he also understood the mysteries of navigation and the fine art of sailing. It is doubtful if Hamer himself boasted either of these accomplishments. In any case, within thirty-six days after boarding the *Eagle,* James Cook found himself promoted to the important post of master's mate. Here was a rank as high as that which John Walker had offered, while warning him that if he joined the Royal Navy he would be forced to start all over again at the bottom of the ladder. If Cook was elated at such swift promotion, he made no entry of it in the diary he habitually kept up during his off-watch. Perhaps in calm self-confidence he accepted this rise in fortune as his just due.

Captain Hamer had been ordered to patrol a turbulent reach of water that stretched from Land's End to the southernmost tip of Ireland. He was to engage in action any French vessel sighted. In pursuit of this duty, the *Eagle* ran into a storm of hurricane force, suffering so much damage that Hamer deemed it advisable to put back into Plymouth for repairs.

In Plymouth he dallied through the fine months of summer, while James Cook fumed silently at such incompetence. It appeared that Captain Hamer had no stomach for the dangerous business of blockade. When at last word of the unnecessary delay reached the Lords of the Admiralty, the *Eagle's* captain was promptly relieved of command. Here was one of those lucky incidents that studded like stars the career of James Cook; for the man who replaced the cowardly Hamer was Sir Hugh Palliser.

Himself a Yorkshireman, Palliser was destined in good time to become governor of Newfoundland, and a Lord of the Admiralty. He recognized at once the extraordinary qualities that marked the character of the young Master's Mate. Despite the differences of background that ordinarily would have stood between an English baronet and a farmer's son, the two men formed the beginnings of a lifelong friendship. It was Sir Hugh Palliser who in later years helped to promote James Cook from one height to another.

The months flew past. By May of 1756 the conflict between England and France—simmering for centuries—burst into open flame. The Seven Years' War was officially declared. Within a year the *Eagle* was to gain fame when it surprised and attacked the fifty-gun French East Indiaman, *Duc d'Aquitaine*. The English ship emerged victorious from the conflict, but so nearly a total wreck as barely to reach Plymouth with all hands laboring at the pumps.

James Cook understood that the *Eagle's* condition meant weeks, perhaps months, ashore, superintending repairs in drydock. It was not for this purpose that he had enlisted in the Royal Navy. Swift as his promotion had been, he was filled with impatience at the thought of the long upward climb he still must make. Someday he would wear a lieutenant's uniform or a commander's. Perhaps even a captain's! But time was of the utmost importance. Already the first year of his enlistment had stretched into a second. He determined to ask for transfer to a ship in action.

Seated in the *Eagle's* after-cabin, with the ports closed to mute the hammering of the ship's carpenters, Sir Hugh Palliser stared thought-

fully at the young man who faced him. Palliser
liked what he saw: the level eyes as clear as sea
water; the bold nose; the squared-off chin; the
head so finely set on a strong column of throat.
Yes, James Cook was a man to win admiration
and inspire confidence.

"So you wish to be transferred, eh?" Palliser
demanded.

"I do, sir," came the impatient answer. "Any
good carpenter or blacksmith can put the *Eagle*
into fighting trim again. But that'll take months
and there's a war being fought. I'd like to be in
it, sir. Besides, I'm a fish out of water ashore!"

Palliser permitted himself a smile. Though
James Cook never presumed on their friendship,
nor crossed the rigid line that divides a ship's
captain from a master's mate, the two men understood and admired each other. The Captain
cocked one eyebrow, quizzically. "Had you
thought, perhaps, of another promotion?" he
asked.

Cook's eyes kindled. "I've thought of nothing
else, sir."

"I had an idea 'twas so! How old are you?"

"Twenty-nine, sir."

"Not too old for what I have in mind." Pal-

The Eagle *attacked the French vessel,* Duc d'Aquitaine

liser glanced up quickly. "What would you say if I recommended you for a master's warrant in the *Pembroke?*"

A jaw less firm than James Cook's would have dropped in surprise. The *Pembroke* was one of nineteen ships of the line under Admiral Boscawen, being made ready to attack the French in Canada. For a man still in his twenties, an appointment as sailing master in such a ship would be in the nature of a triumph.

"Do you—mean it, sir?" Cook managed.

Hugh Palliser frowned in mock severity. "I do not talk, young man, to hear the sound of my voice. I promise you this: if you will contain your impatience for a bit longer, I shall recommend you for promotion without delay. You are ready for a master's rating. Indeed, you have earned it."

Both men came to their feet. Behind the surface of their words ran a current of feeling.

"The *Eagle* will miss your services," Palliser was saying slowly, "and so shall I. Your place will not be easy to fill. But in all truth it would be unfair to delay your advance. Already you have gone higher in the King's service than most seamen aspire."

"I have been rarely fortunate," the other protested. "Fortunate in knowing men like you. How can I express my thanks, sir?" The words came from the fullness of James Cook's heart.

"No need to thank me," Hugh Palliser answered. "I have a notion that one day it will be England who thanks *you*. The world stands aside for a man who knows where he is going. Good luck and Godspeed, my friend."

With a grip of the hand, with the flash of a smile, they parted.

Regardless of James Cook's impatience, the affairs of nations moved ponderously. The blockade dragged on. Hugh Palliser made good his promise: Cook received his warrant as sailing master of the *Pembroke* in October of 1757. Yet a full year elapsed before Admiral Boscawen's squadron stood assembled in the crowded harbor of Plymouth. William Pitt's plan to strike directly at the French colonies in Canada had been forced to wait until a fleet of new vessels had been built; for while the war would be waged in North America, the blockade of France must be maintained.

At last the hour was ripe. For James Cook

this was a thrilling moment. The very thought of what the New World stood for kindled his imagination. Any thoughtful man could see that Europe was old and wearing out; but the vast continent across the ocean—so little known, with resources scarcely tapped—was a prize of the first water. The nation who won that prize would become the most powerful on earth.

February was a bad month for crossing the Atlantic, but that couldn't be helped. Gales and contrary winds beset the fleet. Icebergs were an ever-present danger. The ships of the squadron became separated, and the young Sailing Master of the *Pembroke* was forced to employ every wile and skill of navigation that he knew. A crossing which ordinarily would have taken two or three weeks consumed eleven.

But this was the least of James Cook's tribulations. Scurvy—that dread disease of long voyages—crept like a horror through the laboring ship. Eleven weeks without fresh food or water, in bitter cold, with never a chance of dry clothes or bedding, began to take toll of the crew. To the Sailing Master's consternation, one by one his men faltered. Their joints swelled, the bones of arms or legs often snapping under the slightest exertion. Their gums bled, their teeth fell out; and a great weakness overtook so many of them that the simplest order was performed with difficulty.

Here was a major calamity, for scurvy could wreck a ship just as surely as reef or gale. But it was a problem that James Cook's inquisitive mind at once examined. Dire as the situation was, this was the beginning of what years later would prove to be his greatest contribution to seafaring: the conquest of scurvy.

Why, he demanded of himself, was the ordinary seaman more often afflicted than a ship's officer? Could scurvy be caused by the conditions under which the men were forced to live in the fo'c'sle? How well Cook understood those conditions! In the merchant service, where voyages were short and a crew fared better, the disease was much less prevalent than in the Navy. In the King's service the seamen lived for months on end on salt pork pickled in bloody brine, the only other staple being hardtack, often alive with weevils. The drinking water grew foul to the taste and the casks that contained it were known as "harness casks," on account of the water's brown color. Then there was the vermin of

the fo'c'sle, brought aboard in the rags of jail-
birds and beggars, and the brutal custom of flogging for the slightest misdemeanor. All these
sapped a man's strength and left him easy prey
to disease.

On the other hand, the table of the officers
groaned under a weight of hams, cheeses,
smoked beef, pickled eggs, fruit cakes and fine
wines. Only on the longest voyages, when all supplies were reaching an end, did scurvy make its
appearance among the officers.

Yes, there could be no doubt about it—insuf-
ficient food and foul quarters were the causes
of scurvy. And at the back of James Cook's
questing mind a plan began to form. Someday
he would experiment in preserving foods—vegetables and fruits. Why couldn't carrots and beans
and peas and apples be dried and kept indefinitely? Surely men in sound health could better
resist illness.

The seed of an idea new to seafarers had
fallen in rich soil. One day it would bear fruit.

In the meantime, twenty-nine members of the
Pembroke's crew were buried overside, while
more than twice that number were incapable of
duty. When at last the far dim headlands of

Canada were sighted by the lookout, to a harassed sailing master named James Cook the New World looked as welcome as the Promised Land.

The winter of 1759 was the severest that the colonials had yet experienced in America. By spring, when Admiral Sir Charles Saunders arrived from England to assist General Wolfe in forcing the enemy's surrender, ice still flecked the mouth of the St. Lawrence River.

Wolfe had conceived the bold plan of sailing the English fleet straight up the river to Quebec, thus taking Montcalm by surprise. For the French were confident that ships of the line were too large and unwieldy to negotiate the labyrinth of rocks and rapids in the St. Lawrence. There were no charts except those held by the French themselves. Obviously the region must be surveyed and soundings taken before Saunders' fleet could move into action. But such a task as surveying the treacherous river (under the very guns of the enemy) called for courage in the face of danger, steady nerves, and skill in the painstaking craft of chart-making. Where was such a man to be found? Few English naval officers could read charts, let alone make them.

Sir Charles Saunders sent at once for James Cook.

Though the latter knew the Admiral by repute, this was the first time he had stood in the presence of that remarkable man. Saunders had served as first lieutenant with the great Anson on a circumnavigation of the world. Honors had been showered upon him, yet he had none of the bombast of the quarter-deck. He and James Cook were hewn from the same hard substance. They liked each other immediately. And Cook felt the tingling excitement, the tension, which warned him that again he stood at an important crossroads of his life.

The Admiral came at once to the point. "I've heard much about you, Cook," he said, "from Hugh Palliser."

Palliser . . . His old friend! James Cook smiled. "Only good reports, I trust, sir."

A grin cracked the Admiral's weathered cheek. "You may depend on it. Among his recommendations, Palliser told me you understand surveying and map-making."

The other hesitated. "I have studied surveying. But I don't pretend to know more than a bit, sir."

"Blast me!" Saunders exclaimed. "Even a bit is more than the rest of us know. The French have destroyed all buoys and markers in the river. Soundings must be taken and charts made before the fleet can move on Quebec. The job is yours, Cook—and a devilish, dangerous one it is, too. It can be done only at night, for the French are in league with the Indians and *they* have eyes like a hawk." The man's fist knotted. "Come back with those charts—even if you leave your scalp behind!"

Cook clicked his heels. "I shall do my best, sir."

The Admiral relaxed, chuckled. "Palliser told me, if I remember correctly, that your best is good enough for anyone. I neglected to ask him, however, about your training. You would have been much younger than I at the Royal Academy of Science or I should have remembered you. You studied there, of course?"

"No, sir. I did not."

The Admiral's brows came up. "Indeed? Then what *is* your schooling?"

With level eyes James Cook looked back at his superior officer. Between them stood the chasm of high birth and fine family, of wealth and naval tradition. But there was quiet pride, the honest conviction of a man who knows his true worth, in Cook's voice as he answered, "Since my twelfth year, I am self-taught, sir."

Saunders pursed his lips to whistle. "By the Powers!" he exclaimed. "Extraordinary! Never have I heard the like." Admiration shone in his eyes and the pressure of his hand was firm as he closed grips with the younger man. "Well, *well!* All success to you, Cook. And remember—the fate of the squadron and every man aboard depends on how well you carry out your mission."

"I shan't forget. Depend on it, sir."

Treading on air, James Cook left the Admiral's presence. He knew his shortcomings in the field of surveying, but he felt in his bones that he would not fail. At every crisis in his life, some power—luck, chance, call it what you will —had helped him through. But for the first time he understood that he had never waited for luck. He had always been ready when opportunity came. And he vowed that he would never rest until he had learned as much as possible about surveying and charting. As for danger— to him danger was as meat and wine to a man who is starving.

To the tips of his fingers James Cook felt vibrant and alive. Ah, life had been good to him!

Some ten miles from Quebec the St. Lawrence narrowed; and in its center (at the eastern end of the Ile d'Orleans) were numerous rocky and treacherous islets. Here the channel which followed the river's northern bank passed over to the south, through what was called the Traverse —a stretch of water dangerous in the extreme, and opposite the camp where the French army was entrenched. Saunders' plan was to sail his squadron under the very guns of the enemy batteries, in order to bombard them and cover the advance of Wolfe's army. The accuracy with which James Cook must carry out his mission was of vital importance. If he failed, the fleet would be jeopardized and Canada might be forever lost to England.

The tall lean man who stood at the river's edge that dark night, giving final instructions to his two picked oarsmen, was well aware both of the danger he faced and of the great prize at stake. But James Cook's hand was steady, his

voice firm as he climbed into the stern of a dinghy and gave the order to shove off.

There was no moon, but in the dark bowl of
the sky stars hung like jewels. On all sides the
high forest loomed black against the star glitter,
and the mysterious river whispered as it moved
from one oblivion into another. All the world
seemed to hold its breath with listening. Not far
away the eyes of some nocturnal animal gleamed
with green fire for an instant, then vanished.
Cook's lips tightened. Even now other eyes, keen
and Indian, might be following his every movement. . . .

"Steady, men," he cautioned in low tone.
"Muffle those oarlocks! Bear larboard, there—"

He gripped the steering oar with sure hands
and stared ahead. From somewhere deep in the
forest came the hushed, rhythmic murmur of
drums—a sound felt rather than heard, striking
the entrails rather than the ear. Cook could hear
the quickened breathing of the oarsmen; and
in the gathering tension of night and danger,
he felt every faculty coil in upon itself like a
spring of steel. The dark current caught the dinghy and swept it into midstream.

A lead plummet had been attached to a strong

light line and marked off in fathoms. Lashing
the steering oar, Cook dropped the line over the
stern sheets into the water, lowering it gradually
until the weight reached bottom. He sounded the
river at ten-yard intervals. He took observations
by the stars and jotted his notes, almost by instinct, on scraps of paper he could hardly see.
Nothing escaped his sharp eye or evaded his
phenomenal memory.

Not until the third night did the enemy's Indian scouts detect him. By then the work was
done—in the very nick of time! Even as Cook's
men headed the dinghy down river, a swarm of
canoes could be seen shoving off from the dark
shore. The canoes were filled with shouting savages.

"Quick, men!" Cook cried. "They're after us!
Pull for your lives!"

The oarsmen strained for all they were worth.
The light craft sped across the currents. The wet
blades of the oars flashed in the starlight. But
one backward glance convinced Cook that the
canoes were gaining. His heart thumped. The
wild cries of the Indians came louder and
louder, making him tighten his grip on the
steering oar. And in that second he seemed to

hear again the Admiral's voice, saying, "Come back with those charts—even if you leave your scalp behind!"

"Pull, lads!" he urged. "We'll beat them yet! We're almost ashore—"

The men made a last heroic effort. The dinghy thudded into the river bank. Cook and his companions sprang ashore and darted into the black shelter of the forest. Behind them the Indians could be heard yelling wildly as they beached their canoes. A shower of arrows whined through the air. An arrowhead ripped a sleeve of Cook's jacket and buried itself quivering in a tree.

But luck was on the side of the white men. By some miracle they succeeded in giving the savages the slip. They reached the camp where General Wolfe had set up headquarters. From his pocket, safe and dry and wrapped in oiled silk, James Cook produced a record of the observations and soundings he had taken.

Several days later his completed charts were laid before the English commanders. Neither Saunders nor Wolfe nor Cook himself could have guessed that, so accurately had the job been done, his charts would be used by pilots of the St. Lawrence for generations to come.

The rest is history. More than two hundred fighting ships of the English fleet ran the dangerous rapids of the Traverse without a single casualty. The battle that followed was long and bloody. But by mid-September Wolfe had scaled the Plains of Abraham and the city of Quebec had fallen.

Once again Sir Charles Saunders sent for the young Sailing Master. The difference in rank between the two men momentarily vanished in the warmth of the Admiral's greeting.

"You must know, young man," Saunders said solemnly, "that our success in defeating the enemy has been due in part to your efforts. You did splendid work, Cook, in the face of great danger."

James Cook shifted his weight. He was never easy under praise. Besides, he felt that he had only done his duty. "There are places in the Thames, sir," he murmured, "fully as dangerous as the St. Lawrence."

"But not with Indians and Frenchmen popping at you," the other retorted. "You are far too modest, my fellow, for your own good. Mark my words, if you don't make a sputter about what you've done, you'll get no credit from the Admiralty."

Lamely the other answered, "I fear, sir, that I am a sorry failure as a sputterer."

"Then I shall sputter for you," the Admiral stated. "The service you have done England shall be brought to the attention of the Lords of the Admiralty. I may add, it will do you no harm."

"Thank you, sir."

"Oh, and one matter more—the *Pembroke* is returning to England, but there will be great need of your services as a map-maker here in Canada. I have given orders for your appointment to the flagship *Northumberland,* under Lord Colville."

Here was a stroke of luck indeed! Lord Colville was one of the most powerful men in the Royal Navy. Overcome at such good fortune, James Cook could only mumble his gratitude and beat an awkward retreat.

5 The Great Adventure

Through the open window of his lodgings in Shadwell, not far from London Bridge, a brisk wind brought the smell of the Thames to James Cook's nostrils. How good it was to be back again in London after four years of the American wilderness. He had applied for his discharge from the Navy; but he had been so long afloat that the floor seemed to pitch and roll beneath his feet like the deck of a ship.

For a moment there flashed through the young man an awareness of all that had happened during the years he had been away from England. The French had surrendered their Canadian provinces. Lord Colville had written a glowing letter to the Admiralty, urging that Cook's nautical charts be published at once. Out of his term of service Cook had saved some 300 pounds sterling—a handsome sum, half of which he promptly sent to his aging parents in Great Ayton. As a surveyor he had every reason to take pride in his achievement; but it was with impatience that the young man turned away from the window. Achievement was empty indeed when a man had no one with whom to share it! Not having won a commission in the Navy, he was accepted on sufferance by the officers, while his rank as sailing master raised a wall between himself and the ordinary seamen. Except for his friendship with Hugh Palliser, James Cook had been made painfully aware of his aloneness within a world of his fellows.

There came a knock at the door. That would

be his landlady, the amiable Mrs. Batts, whose motherly eye saw to his comfort.

"Come in!" he called.

But it was Elizabeth, his landlady's daughter, who entered the room. The young man's heart skipped a beat at sight of the shy, dark-eyed girl.

"I didn't expect *you*," he said.

"Mother is ailing," the girl explained quietly. "She charged me to see that you have fresh linen and that your room is dusted."

Though James Cook had faced many dangers and looked with a steady eye on peril, this slim, soft-voiced girl threw him into confusion. "You are more than kind," he stammered.

Elizabeth arranged the towels in a neat row above the washbowl and pitcher. Then she ran her fingers over a pile of books stacked on the worktable. "No dust!" she stated, inspecting one fingertip in surprise.

The man smiled, feeling suddenly more at ease. "My books seldom have a chance to gather dust," he told her. "They're always in use."

The girl's glance lingered with admiration on a row of charts fastened to the wall. "That is your own work?" she queried, on a note of wonder.

The other nodded. "The Admiralty is publishing them soon." And for the first time James Cook felt a surge of pride in what, single-handed, he had accomplished. Something within him that had been remote and cold glowed in the warmth of Elizabeth's admiration. It was like ice thawing in the springtime.

"Oh, to be able to do such things!" the girl cried. "How dull the rest of us must seem to you. Tell me—is it truly wonderful, that Canadian wilderness?"

The young man's teeth flashed white. His voice was eager as he exclaimed, "There's bigness in that country! You can hear the whistle of the bull elk when the first snow flurries fall, and the bears come out in broad day after the settlers' livestock. And the trees grow so thick that God Almighty would have to take an axe to them if He wanted to see the sky He made." James Cook paused, breathless. For him this was a long speech.

"Shall you be returning soon to Canada?" The girl's question seemed to hold a meaning beyond the words themselves. Could it be that Elizabeth did not want him to go away?

James Cook shook his head; and then he turned toward the window, his eyes alight with some far vision. "There are too many other places in the world still to be discovered," he said, almost as if he were thinking aloud.

Ruefully the girl answered, "I've heard that some men are like the ships they sail—never content for long with the home port, always seeking some new horizon."

"Perhaps I am one such," the other confessed. "But remember—after the longest journey every ship comes to final anchor."

"True, but how lonely for those who await the home-coming ships."

"That is the lot of a woman who marries a sailor, Elizabeth." Her name seemed to come naturally to his lips.

Now it was the girl's turn to be confused. A rosy flush crept up her cheek. "I must go," she murmured.

But as she turned away, the man caught her hands in both his own. He felt their fluttering birdlike pulse and his own pulse leaped in re-

sponse. "I'll see you soon again?" he begged. "Please—"

"Perhaps," Elizabeth gasped. "Yes! Yes, surely!" She snatched her hands from his and hurried toward the open door.

One month later, on December 21, 1762, wedding bells pealed in the Parish Church of Little Barking for James Cook and his beloved Elizabeth. They bought a house in Mile End Road, east of the stir and bustle of London, and it seemed as if the young husband's seafaring days might well be over.

But not for long. His old friend Sir Hugh

Palliser had been appointed governor of New-foundland and Labrador. The little-known colony, with its fogbound coasts, must be mapped. Palliser sent, of course, for James Cook.

Thus, barely four months after his marriage, the young man found himself once more pacing the quarter-deck of a ship, while Elizabeth set herself patiently to learn the lonely lesson of the woman who weds a man of the sea.

For James Cook, his experience in Newfoundland would have far-reaching results. Not long after his arrival, an eclipse of the sun took place. He wrote a detailed report of the phenomenon and submitted it to the Royal Society of London. So skillfully had he presented his observations that the learned scientists were astounded. Who, they asked, *was* this James Cook? What was his scientific training? Their astonishment grew apace when they discovered the facts. How did it happen that such a man, after eleven years of distinguished service in the Royal Navy, held no commission as an officer? Something, they muttered, should be done about it!

But the mission to Newfoundland consumed five long and lonely years, and James Cook was

nearing forty. Like a weight, the conviction settled on him that he would never become an officer now. Commissions were for gentlemen's sons,
for the high-placed and mighty—not for men
whose forebears had tilled the fields of England.
And for the first time he reflected bitterly how
much wiser it might have been had he never left
Great Ayton. The light of his lucky star, in
which he had believed so fervently, seemed to
flicker and grow pale.

Some years earlier, an English astronomer
named Halley had predicted that the comet
which bears his name would be visible in 1759.
To everyone's astonishment the comet had appeared on schedule. Consequently, when Halley
asserted that the planet Venus would pass between the earth and the sun in the year 1769,
no one doubted the prediction. If observations
of the transit of Venus could be made simultaneously from several different points on the
globe, the age-old question of the sun's distance
from the earth could be computed exactly. This
would help solve the navigator's problem of
reckoning "longitude," which, up to that time,
was still troublesome.

It was in November of 1767 that James Cook returned finally to England. In that same month the Royal Society began to lay plans to observe the eclipse which Halley predicted would take place two years hence. The plan was to send two scientific expeditions to the South Seas, two to Europe, and two to northern Canada. To head the Pacific expedition the Society already had chosen its man: a Scot named Alexander Dalrymple. It was he who still believed in the existence of a great southern continent containing 50,000,000 people.

James Cook was asked to pick out a ship suitable for such an enterprise. True to his first love, he chose a North Sea collier built at Whitby —a sturdy craft of 370 tons christened the *Endeavour*. Cook would have given his right hand to sail on the expedition. But Dalrymple, in addition to being a Fellow of the Royal Society, was the brother of a lord. Only James Cook seemed to be disturbed by the fact that the man, though a respected scientist, had never been to sea! Truly the ways of the Admiralty were difficult to fathom.

It was at this point that Alexander Dalrymple played directly into James Cook's hands. Not content with being the leader of a scientific expedition, the man demanded an officer's rating in the Royal Navy. The First Lord of the Admiralty, Sir Edward Hawke, was outraged. The *Endeavour,* purchased by public funds, belonged properly to the Navy. Never, Sir Edward declared angrily, would a King's ship be commanded by a civilian!

But Dalrymple remained obdurate. He would have the whole cake or none. It looked as if the entire plan would collapse. With the transit of Venus little more than a year distant, the Royal Society was in a flutter of consternation. Who was capable of leading such an expedition into the South Seas? Suddenly one of the learned scientists remembered James Cook's brilliant report of the eclipse in Newfoundland. Here was the man! Sir Hugh Palliser leaped instantly to champion the cause of his friend. Lord Colville did likewise.

And thus the matter was decided. Why, everyone asked, hadn't they thought of Cook in the first place? Of all the veterans of the Navy, none had his wide range of experience and knowledge.

To James Cook and Elizabeth it was little short of a miracle that the son of a Yorkshire farmer, who a score of times had been passed over for promotion, should be given the most enviable command in England. Cook remembered the long years when, in preparation for this very moment, he had pushed his aching body and tired mind to the limits of endurance. But in his hour of triumph he was humble.

Elizabeth would not allow herself to think of the dangers that lay in wait for her husband. She had watched the light leap in his eyes when he received his commission as lieutenant; that light must never grow dim again. How handsome he was, so tall and straight in his new blue uniform with the gilt braid and white cuffs, the snowy stock at his neck, the cocked hat!

"How proud I am of you," she whispered. "But, oh, how happy I shall be when I learn that your ship is on the homeward course."

The man bent his head to hers. "You must not be afraid for me, my Elizabeth. Surely you know that I was born under a lucky star?"

"And I hitched my wagon to that star, my husband." She smiled bravely, turning her head aside so that he should not see her tears.

Tenderly the man embraced her. "Would you have it otherwise?"

Low and sure came Elizabeth's answer. "Not for worlds! God watch over you, my dearest one, and bring you home to me."

The *Endeavour* lay at Deptford on the Thames. Never did a vessel flying the broad flag of England look less like a King's ship. Her length was ninety-eight feet, her beam twenty-nine. With bluff bows, a stern square and high, she looked like what she was: a cargo vessel built to carry a load through any kind of sea. James Cook knew her value. For his purpose you couldn't beat a North Country ship.

Since the expedition enjoyed the blessing of the King, no expense was spared in outfitting. The *Endeavour* was provisioned for a voyage of two years. She was armed with carronades and swivel guns. Spare canvas, spars, cordage and timber were stored below. There was a goodly supply of trinkets for trading with the savages. The crew of officers and men numbered seventy-two, with twelve additional marines. Three scientists joined the party: Charles Green, an eminent astronomer; Sir Joseph Banks, a wealthy young aristocrat who had made a name for himself as a botanist; and a Swedish naturalist

named Dr. Solander. James Cook worked tirelessly, his keen eye missing nothing. He spared neither his men nor himself. But it was the end of summer before all was in readiness for departure. Cook took his last farewell of the home in Mile End Road. How much would happen to him before he held Elizabeth in his arms again!

The wharf at Plymouth was jammed with spectators and festive with bunting. Wives and sweethearts wept to see their men embarking for the unknown. A southeasterly breeze whipped

Spectators jammed the wharf to watch the ship set out

across the water as sail after snowy sail was sheeted home and hoisted. One by one the mooring lines were cast off. With a rousing chantey the seamen strained at the capstan bars. There came a hiss of spray thrown back by the cutwater as the *Endeavour*—with bowsprit pointed south and a cloud of gulls screaming at the masthead—set out on her great adventure.

The day was August 26th, the year, 1768.

6   Lieutenant Cook

Eighteen days later, overladen though she was, the *Endeavour* dropped anchor off Madeira. Here the sea claimed its first victim. While weighing anchor, the master's mate became entangled with the hawser and was dragged down by the anchor fluke. The man was drowned before he could be rescued. Superstitious sailors saw this as an omen of bad fortune. The *En-*

deavour, they muttered, would never again sight the green hills of England.

But by mid-November this dark prediction was forgotten. Rio de Janeiro had dropped astern and the ship was racing south with all sail set. An island called Tahiti, in the Pacific Ocean, had been chosen as the ideal place to observe the transit of Venus. In Tahiti during nine months of the year the skies were invariably clear. But first there was Cape Horn to be reckoned with, and many a long week would pass before the *Endeavour* dipped her bows into the wide Pacific. James Cook faced confidently ahead. He commanded a good ship and a fine crew. The scientists, Banks in particular, were proving to be excellent passengers. Still, there were moments when he could hardly believe his good luck in leading one of the greatest enterprises of his century. There had been nothing like it since Columbus, almost three hundred years earlier, had sailed west to discover a new world.

"Land ho! Land ho-o-o!"

The electrifying cry brought all hands on deck. Sailors went swarming up the rigging.

Cook squinted anxiously through his spyglass. Far off to starboard lay land—bleak and snow-covered, with columns of volcanic smoke rising heavily in the air. The sky was sullen and the edges of the lower clouds were tinged with a fiery glow. Dr. Solander and Joseph Banks joined the Captain on the quarter-deck.

"There it is, gentlemen," Cook stated. "Tierra del Fuego—Land of Fire. And right where it's supposed to be."

" 'Pon my soul," Banks exclaimed, "Magellan couldn't have thought of a better name! Looks like the Devil's own caldron."

All hands agreed that Tierra del Fuego was a forbidding and inhospitable shore. To the east of the mainland proper lay a rocky island; between the two was the passage known as LeMaire Strait. A ship must pass through that dangerous stretch of water in order to round Cape Horn. The cold grew ever more searching and ice formed on spars and rigging as the *Endeavour* sailed along the bleak coast. The ship was still carrying every permissible rag of canvas, and under the tremendous pressure she bucked and staggered. Water boiled white along her half-submerged lee bulwarks.

Wrapped in his great-cloak and braced in a corner of the taffrail, James Cook gauged his ship's performance. He was determined to hang onto all possible sail. As the *Endeavour* entered LeMaire Strait, she was beset on every side. Winds that boxed the compass took her aback. Giant seas burst over her bows, to rush aft in avalanches of foam. But it was in just such a ship as this, in the treacherous offshore waters of the North Sea, that James Cook had learned his trade. The confident shout of his voice, his calm and indomitable face, reassured those who faltered and put new strength into the weak. Who could be afraid with such a man at the helm?

The passage of LeMaire Strait consumed four storm-tossed days—breaking all previous records. And somehow Cook found time to make a chart of the coastline and set down his sailing observations with unfailing accuracy.

Fresh water was now the crying need. Toward that end the ship dropped anchor in a sheltered bay. The casks were sent ashore for refilling. The scientists, headed by Dr. Solander, determined to explore a mountain visible in the distance and to bring back any strange plant or animal life that might be discovered. Ten men made up the exploring party—the very backbone of the Royal Society's expedition. With some concern Cook watched them make their preparations, for it had begun to snow heavily and no man could say what dangers lurked in this unknown, savage land.

"I shall have a gun fired at four o'clock of the afternoon watch," Cook informed Banks. "You will reply by musket, if you please. By all means make sure to be back aboard ship before dark."

"You may rely on it, Lieutenant," Joseph Banks assured the other; but his eyes were shining with the far-off, mystic look of the true scientist—a fact which increased Cook's concern. If only there could have been one man of sound sense among those learned gentlemen! But the scientific party was not bound by Cook's authority. He could only fret in silence and watch them depart.

Throughout the afternoon the storm increased. Soon it was impossible to see farther than a cable's length from the bow of the ship. A wild wind shrilled through the rigging. Hourly the Captain's anxiety increased. At four o'clock

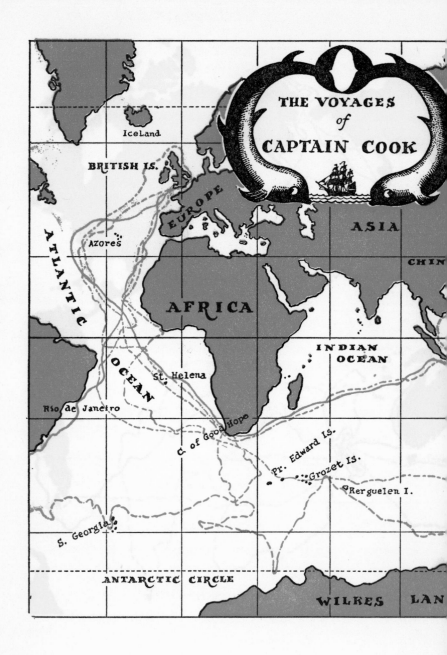

THE VOYAGES
of
CAPTAIN COOK

Iceland

BRITISH IS.

EUROPE

ASIA

Azores

CHIN

ATLANTIC

AFRICA

INDIAN
OCEAN

St. Helena

OCEAN

Rio de Janeiro

C. of Good Hope

Pr. Edward Is.

Crozet Is.

Kerguelen I.

S. Georgia

ANTARCTIC CIRCLE

WILKES LAN

he ordered the gun to be fired. No answering signal could be heard. A second *boom* from the swivel, then a third, met with the same ominous silence.

"They're done for," the bosun muttered, "every last one of 'em. Frozen stiff as an anchor, like as not."

Angrily Cook silenced the speaker, but the words found an echo in his heart.

Mr. Hicks, the first officer, shared his superior's anxiety. "Shall I organize a searching party, sir, while it's still light?" he suggested.

"Not by a long chalk! It would be dark before you got a mile inland." Cook's voice was edgy with anger at himself. If disaster overtook the party, it was no one's fault but his own. Right or wrong, as ship's captain he should have imposed his authority upon the scientists. God willing, this would not happen again!

"There's no telling in what direction they may have wandered," he added heavily. "It would be foolhardy to risk the lives of others in such a storm."

Reluctantly Hicks agreed. All night long the two men kept tireless vigil, while red signal flares burned on the fo'c'sle head. Just at daybreak, somewhere off to the east, a single ragged shot could be heard above the howling of the wind.

"They're alive!" The cry burst from a score of throats.

But it was eight men, rather than ten, who returned to the ship—men nearer dead than alive. The tale Banks had to tell strengthened Cook's conviction to keep, in future, a strong hand on these visionaries.

In their passage toward the distant mountain, the scientists had blundered into a half-frozen bog. There a heavy snowstorm swept down upon them. They discovered a few natives huddling in the crudest of shelters, but were driven off fiercely by these wretched people. Shortly afterward, one of the scientists was seized by an epileptic fit and given up for lost (he later recovered, however). Two of Banks' men insisted on lying down in the snow. Nothing could stop them. They preferred death to further struggle. Half frozen, the other eight men trudged on through the night to keep warmth in their miserable bodies. By dawn they discovered the red flares of the *Endeavour* and found that they had been walking in a wide circle. Another hour and they would surely all have perished. But in spite of everything, Joseph Banks (true scientist that he was) had managed to collect a kind of wild celery and to kill a land fowl of unknown species.

With vast relief James Cook gave the order to weigh anchor. He was glad to be quit of this dismal place. By January 22nd, almost five months after leaving England, the *Endeavour* showed her heels to Tierra del Fuego—land of fire and snow.

Six days later she had doubled Cape Horn and entered the Pacific Ocean—another record-breaking performance. Men's spirits soared with the changing weather. Gone was the world of icy winds and mountainous waves. The ship's course was laid northwest, across seas unbelievably blue. Schools of dolphins capered about the bowsprit, while now and again a whale heaved its varnished hulk to the surface to throw a jet of rainbow mist high into the air. The sky was alive with sea birds—petrels, terns, frigates— and on effortless wings the kingly albatross soared above them all.

At night the men slung their hammocks on deck, while the trade wind strummed through the rigging, lulling them to sleep like songs half remembered from childhood. And sometimes, checking his ship's position by the bright stars of the tropics, James Cook thought of Elizabeth keeping her lonely vigil. At such moments invariably he sighed, forcing his thoughts into safer channels. He wondered what Tahiti would be like. . . . Captain Wallis, of H.M.S. *Dolphin,* had touched there some years before and sang loud praise of the beautiful island and its handsome people. But Cook well knew that to men weary of the sea such a place could be a breeding ground for mutiny or desertion.

With as little change as comes from morning passing into afternoon, February drifted into March. By the fifth of April—just when it seemed as if this voyage had had no beginning and would have no end—there sounded the lookout's thrilling cry: "Land ho! Land ho-o-o!"

Tahiti! The island was so distant that it appeared to be no more than a deeper stain of the morning sky—the merest supposition of land. Between sea and sky it hung in timeless suspension, and the *Endeavour* bore smartly down upon it.

James Cook stood on the quarter-deck, his legs wide-braced more from habit than from need, since there was no swell or roll as the ship clipped across the equatorial currents. In his hand he held Wallis's chart of the island, and it was with some satisfaction that, in taking sights, he was able to mark a correction on the chart. In Cook's opinion, Wallis was an amiable gentleman but something of a duffer when it came to navigation!

The scientists were grouped around the Captain, while the foremast hands clambered like monkeys up the rigging. As the sun rose, the island assumed more distinct shape—lofty green peaks, shadowy valleys, waterfalls that caught the sunlight and turned into rainbows. It was an apparition taking form before the eyes of the ship's company. So unreal did it appear that they expected to see it dissolve at any moment and vanish in the tranquil light.

"Aye, 'tis a bonny land," Joseph Banks asserted, adding with sly amusement, "Wallis was correct on *that* score, even though he did err as a map-maker."

James Cook restrained a smile as he marked a third correction on the chart.

Mr. Hicks was growling. " 'Tis bonny enough, in all truth. But those green hills were made special for deserters! In such a place 'twill not be easy to keep the men out of trouble."

Cook had been plagued by the same doubt but he remained silent. He'd see to it that afloat or ashore his men were too busy for trouble. Now groves of coconut palms could be seen, sheltering huts of thatch from the sun's fierce glare. Cumulus clouds were reflected in the lagoon beneath the inverted peaks of the mountains, so it seemed as if the fair island lay between two heavens.

Cook's voice rang out, "Stand by to fire a salute!"

The gunner fussed over his swivel cannon. The gun boomed, belched smoke. A thundering echo rolled back from the land.

Then antlike figures could be seen dashing from the thatched houses. Fleets of high-prowed canoes shot like beetles into the water. The whole island seemed to come alive as the *Endeavour* slipped cautiously toward anchorage in Matavai Bay. The ship backed her yards. Wind spilled from the sails as canvas slatted and banged against the spars. There came a grinding rattle as the anchor chain pounded through the hawsehole. The *Endeavor* swung to the running tide and a quietness settled in all her bones.

Now the bay was alive with canoes. The sun flashed on wet paddles, on coppery bodies swinging to the rhythm of a savage chant. Swimmers, decked with flowers, breasted the waves with the ease of seals. A double canoe, roofed with matting, was in the lead. Presently it swung up under the ship's counter.

"That'll be the king, like as not," Mr. Hicks suggested. "Blast me, looks like the royal barge itself!"

And so it proved to be. A half-naked and elderly Polynesian was seated on a raised platform across the two canoes. A second craft bore the queen and her attendants. The *Endeavour* ran up the colors as a royal salute of four guns boomed across the air.

With an agility surprising in one of his years, King Tutaha scrambled up the rope ladder. He swung his legs over the rail and stood there smiling, a man well above the middle height, dressed in a waistcloth of white *tapa*. A necklace of shark's teeth gleamed on his bare brown chest. He had great pride of bearing, even a certain

Fleets of high-prowed canoes shot out toward the ship

nobility that he wore as a heritage from forty generations of chieftain stock. Offering a greeting in the Polynesian manner, Tutaha seized James Cook by the shoulders and rubbed his own nose against that of the astounded Captain. Then at a rasped command an attendant rushed up with a small box made from a gourd. The King spat into the box, taking great care lest one drop of spittle be lost. Reverently the attendant covered the box and bestowed it for safekeeping about his person. No king who had enemies seen and unseen, natural or supernatural, could risk his spittle or nail parings falling into the hands of an ill-wisher.

This accomplished, the King laid a hand on his bare chest. "Me Tutaha," he proclaimed. "Me King Tahiti."

This statement exhausted a fund of English learned, beyond doubt, from Captain Wallis. From that moment until the day of departure three months hence, James Cook and his men would develop the fine art of sign language. Meanwhile, the Queen, weary of awaiting her lord's permission, hoisted her vast bulk up the straining rope ladder. Settled solidly on the quarter-deck, to Cook's discomfiture she also insisted on rubbing noses, smiling happily the while. The handsome Queen's black hair was garlanded with flowers and fell like a cloak almost to her knees. Two copper-colored attendants waved plaited fans above her head while everyone beamed with wide good nature.

"*Ia ora na! Ia ora na outou!*" said the Queen, smiling. This could only be taken to mean, "Welcome!"

Mr. Hicks was heard to mutter to the bosun, "Do you figure these people are cannibals?"

"Can't say," replied the bosun. "But they've got the teeth for it anyhow!"

Quantities of dried fish, breadfruit and bananas were hauled on deck. The royal visitors had not come empty-handed. James Cook produced a bottle of his finest wine and a fruit cake that Elizabeth had packed carefully in tin. Refreshments were exchanged. Both the King and his Queen gagged on the dry cake, while the wine brought tears to their eyes; but they struggled royally to preserve dignity and offer no offense to their hosts. Cook and the scientists, for their part, swallowed manfully as much of the smelly dried fish as they could manage. Thus friendship was cemented. And when at last Tutaha and his Queen took their departure, their gestures indicated that Tahiti and all its bounty lay at the feet of the Englishmen. The first stage of the expedition was a success.

But James Cook understood how readily his sailors, with their rough ways, could offend these simple, childlike people. He must lay down the law at once. On the mainmast he nailed a proclamation for all to see. It stated his orders for good behavior ashore and established rules for trading with the natives. The first sailor to disobey those rules would receive twenty lashes of the "cat." In the Royal Navy, flogging for any misdemeanor was common practice—a custom which sickened James Cook. But the behavior of his men could mean the success or failure of the expedition, and woe unto the man who disobeyed his orders!

That afternoon the Englishmen went ashore for the first time. They were greeted by throngs of Tahitians who waved green branches in token of friendship. Their walk along the beach was like a royal progress. Not far from one arm of Matavai Bay stood the "palace" of the King. This structure was a single long dwelling roofed with thatch. Its walls were of split bamboo through which the wind passed freely. Here King Tutaha and his Queen awaited the return visit of their distinguished guests.

But Cook's active mind was already leaping ahead. He noted that the bay's farther shore offered an excellent site on which to build a fort. Under the protection of the ship's guns the scientific equipment could be set up in preparation for the transit of Venus. To a man of Cook's nature it was exasperating that so much time should be wasted in feasting and pleasantry. By the morrow, he determined, work on the fort should begin at once.

An incident occurred presently which strengthened this determination.

A feast had been prepared for the visitors. Musicians were playing on nose flutes and thumping on drums. At the palace threshold Tutaha greeted the Englishmen with a great show of affection. Soon all were seated on the floor in a circle around a sumptuous meal: roast pig, lobsters, seafood of infinite variety, fruits of all sorts and large bowls of grayish paste called *poi*. Tutaha explained how this latter should be eaten—namely, by scooping up a sticky handful and popping it quickly into the mouth. To the

Englishmen *poi* tasted like so much sour paste. Course followed course, to the tireless monotony of the music. Bowls of *ava* (a rancid beverage made of roots and sea water) were passed from lip to lip with protestations of friendship undying.

Suddenly the revelry was broken by an unmistakable volley of musket shots. Cook stiffened, sprang to his feet. Joseph Banks turned pale beneath his tan. A dreadful silence fell on the gathering. Fear stamped the faces of the Polynesians. The natives who had been grouped outside the palace disappeared as if by magic.

With dismay Cook soon discovered what had happened: half a dozen marines under command of a midshipman had accompanied the landing party ashore. Throughout the feast they had stood by in loose guard. A Tahitian had suddenly snatched a marine's musket and made off with it. The midshipman gave orders to fire. Several natives were wounded. Worse, the thief was pursued and shot dead. By losing his head the midshipman had endangered the lives of the whole party and jeopardized the purpose of the expedition.

No one before had seen James Cook in such a towering rage. The offending officer was at once stripped of rank. Then lamely, with protests of regret and good faith, Cook and his party took their leave of the King and Queen. But the damage had been done. A chill lay like a blight on the Tahitians. The friendship they had offered so generously had been withdrawn. It would take many days to regain their confidence. The afternoon had been a sorry sequel to the morning.

The following day work was begun on the fort. Cook called the chosen sight "Point Venus," in tribute to the planet they had come to observe. An embankment of earth five feet high was thrown up and protected by a moat. Behind the breastworks, in tents, the scientific instruments would be housed. A hundred yards offshore the *Endeavour* lay at anchor, her guns offering ready protection to the fort and to the men at work.

Crowds of curious Tahitians watched the laboring men. The Polynesians' easygoing way of life knew little of manual labor. But one unfortunate trait of native character soon manifested itself: they were clever and unabashed thieves! Knives and hatchets, nails and axes disappeared as if by sleight of hand. Dr. Solander discovered that a shagreen case containing his spectacles had been filched almost from under his nose. The ship's surgeon had been robed of his snuffbox. Tutaha and his court had vanished overnight, thus affording Cook no opportunity for redress.

A somewhat more amusing incident occurred a few days later. Joseph Banks and Dr. Solander had accompanied the Captain on a surveying expedition down the coast. Instead of returning to the fort for the night, Cook and the Doctor decided to sleep in a native's hut, while Banks made himself comfortable in a canoe anchored along shore.

Before going to sleep, Cook removed his stockings and folded them carefully under his head. When he awoke the following morning the stockings had disappeared. Solander was even more unfortunate. That worthy gentleman had lost all his outer clothing. When Banks waded ashore it could be seen that he was wearing only his breeches! His waistcoat, pistol and powder flask had been spirited away while he slept.

Somewhat abashed, the three Englishmen looked at one another ruefully.

"Bless my soul," muttered the good Doctor, "these savages would steal the teeth out of a man's jaw were they loose enough."

"For all their smiling ways," Banks agreed, "they're as light-fingered a set of rogues as you'd meet in a London alley."

But there was worse to come. An event occurred which nearly wrecked the expedition. As the fort drew toward completion, all the scientific instruments were brought ashore, including a quadrant that had been specially constructed for the voyage. This instrument, weighing many pounds, was used in observing the altitude and angular distance of the stars. It was placed in a tent under the special guard of a marine.

The following morning the quadrant had vanished.

The marine had not the slightest idea how the heavy object could have been stolen. James Cook was in despair. The quadrant must be found at once or utter failure be admitted. Fortunately at this point Tutaha returned to the palace. The King seemed anxious to patch up his differences with the Englishmen. With his help the quadrant was finally returned, piece by piece, and put together again. But the identity of the culprit was never revealed.

The last days of May were approaching and the eclipse had been predicted for the third of June. Cook and Solander were to watch the phenomenon from Point Venus, while Banks and a ship's officer sailed across the bay to the island of Moorea to take independent sights.

The long-awaited hour, for which they had sailed half around the world, was at hand. Not a cloud flawed the tropic sky. Eagerly Cook and his companion peered through their telescopes while the great astronomer's clock (in its special tent) ticked off the fateful seconds. In the first flush of morning the dark circle of Venus cut across the edge of the sun. At noon the spreading disc was clearly visible, even to the naked eye. By three o'clock the transit was complete. Cook's figures were checked against those of Joseph Banks. To the best of their ability the Englishmen had fulfilled the Royal Society's mission.

The time for departure had come. Before leaving Tahiti, however, James Cook determined to sail around the entire island, mapping its coast-

line and taking soundings. This he accomplished
with his customary skill. In many ways he felt a
twinge of regret at leaving this beautiful island.
Despite the natives' unfortunate habit of taking
what didn't belong to them, they had great gifts
of humor and generosity and friendship. Their
way of life in that gracious land was idyllic. Indeed, it was this very fact which precipitated an
incident that further delayed the *Endeavour's*
sailing: two marines of the ship's company deserted.

No one knew where to begin searching for
them in the green wilderness of Tahiti. Cook resolved at once on a bold plan. He invited the
King and Queen aboard the ship. All unsuspect-
ing, Tutaha accepted the invitation. Once
aboard, he was informed that unless the deserters
were immediately captured and returned, the
royal family would be held indefinitely as hostages.

It must be remembered that Tahiti is not a
large island, and that all its villages are bound
together by a communication system known as
the "grapevine." When the drums begin to talk
in the hills, messages are being sent with incredible speed from one end of the island to the

other. So it was that when Cook's ultimatum was delivered to the people (who revered their King and Queen) the drums began to rumble. Barely twenty-four hours later the two sheepish marines were discovered in their hiding place in the mountains and brought back to the ship. The royal hostages were at once released, and the order was given to weigh anchor.

Once again, as on the day that the *Endeavour* first had sailed into Matavai Bay, the water was alive with canoes and swimmers. Cook and his men took their last farewells of the Polynesians. Past misunderstandings were forgiven. Gifts were exchanged. Tutaha and his Queen rubbed noses with James Cook, weeping the tears of parting. Paddles were waving. Garlands of flowers floated on the ebbing tide. On shore the na-

tives burst into one of their old-time chants, which was soon drowned out by the rousing chantey of sailors heaving at the capstan bars.

> Wa-ay, up she rises!
> Wa-ay, up she rises!
> Ho, my bullies, yo ho!

Up came the anchor from its bed of coral. The canoes dropped behind. Out across the bay the ship fled like a deer with the hounds at her heels, out through the passage in the barrier reef where the surf on either hand reached hungrily for her as she fled. For a second James Cook glanced astern. The lofty peaks of Tahiti seemed to tower higher and higher, until they struck and split asunder the pearly clouds of morning.

The wide, empty arc of the Pacific stretched ahead. Facing the unknown, the *Endeavour* took her first lift to the grounding swells.

7 The Long Road Home

After leaving Tahiti, the *Endeavour* cruised
among a chain of neighboring islands; but Tahiti
proved to be the largest of the group. In honor
of the Royal Society, Cook christened them the
"Society Islands," then laid a course due south.

Weeks passed, however, before land was again
sighted—seven weeks of empty sea and sky. The

landfall proved to be a far-off range of mysterious mountains which set all hands to guessing. What land could it be? In Joseph Banks's opinion it was Dalrymple's great southern continent.

But James Cook disagreed. "In my belief," he stated, "those are the mountains of New Zealand. Tasman placed them in this same tropic."

"Tasman?" the other queried, with a puzzled frown.

"Aye, the great Dutch navigator. More than a hundred years ago he sighted just such a mountain range south of the tropic of Capricorn."

"Did Tasman go ashore and lay claim to the land?"

"He did not. A swarm of savages turned him back and the Dutch never followed up his discovery."

Banks's eyes lighted. "Then that land—whatever it is—belongs to the country which claims it?"

"You take the words right off my tongue, sir."

Long ago James Cook had made himself familiar with every published account of this part of the Pacific. Not only had he read Tasman's journals, he had all but memorized that Dutchman's sketchy charts. Yes, in Cook's belief that distant landfall was New Zealand.

Presently he became certain of it; for as the *Endeavour* hauled her wind and stood warily in toward the coast, an enormous war canoe shot out from behind a headland, crossing the ship's bows. The craft was fully seventy feet long and decorated with outlandish symbols. The paddlers themselves resembled Tahitians except that their bodies were hideously tattooed. Threatening shouts burst from their lips. They brandished their paddles in a warlike manner.

"Tasman described just such a race of men," Cook insisted. "Who could blame him for not going ashore? I'll wager that craft is as seaworthy as the *Endeavour* and can sail as easily into the wind."

He did not add that its man power would ensure faster progress; for the war canoe held some two hundred warriors—more than twice the number of Cook's men. Here was truly a formidable enemy. The *Endeavour's* swivel guns could hold the canoe at safe distance; but if the range were allowed to close, the savages might easily overpower the Englishmen.

Suddenly a shower of rocks hurled from slingshots hammered against the ship's hull. Some of the missiles, more accurately aimed, struck the deck and felled several sailors. The moment had come to demonstrate the superiority of gunpowder. A volley was fired above the heads of the yelling warriors. Bewildered by the noise as well as by the waterspouts of the four-pound iron cannon balls, the natives of New Zealand quickly brought their great canoe about and headed back for shore. Never had such a mighty thunder reverberated in their hills. Yet there was nothing of timidity in their warlike shouts. They were retreating, yes; but no one doubted they would return to attack.

"You think we shall ever be able to win such a people?" muttered Dr. Solander, dubiously.

"Their weapons are of stone," Cook reminded him. "I saw no evidence of metal among them."

"Meaning," Solander suggested, "that axes and hatchets speak with the tongues of angels?"

"True enough. To a savage one nail is above its weight in pearls. We can only strive for success."

But when, some hours later, a party of men went ashore in the dinghy, they were fiercely repulsed by a shower of spears. The corporal of the marines warned the sailors to fall back and fired over the heads of the savages, who immediately resumed the attack. Far from showing the least fear, one of the natives drew back his spear and aimed it directly at the corporal. A second shot killed the warrior instantly. James Cook was deeply disturbed by this first encounter between his men and the New Zealand natives. Spilling blood was a bad beginning. Where would such tactics end? Orders were given to weigh anchor and a southerly course was laid, but not before the inhospitable spot had first been named "Poverty Bay."

By means of signal smoke, word of the *Endeavour's* presence swept down the coast with the speed of a prairie fire. The marines were constantly on guard and the gunners at battle stations; for behind the headlands of every bay lurked war canoes ready to pounce and do battle. In spite of these dangers, Cook spent hours mapping the coastline—making charts of incomparable accuracy. And always at the back of his mind was the hope that by some good chance he might succeed in gaining the friendship of this splendid, warrior people.

By January a large sheltered bay was discovered where the Englishmen might go ashore without fear of being attacked. This place Cook named "Queen Charlotte Sound," in honor of his King's lady. In this matter he was continuing an established principle. Already he had marked on his charts "Cape Palliser," after his old friend and patron Sir Hugh; "Banks Peninsula," after Sir Joseph; and "Solander Island," in honor of the Swedish scientist—names that would live on through the centuries.

In all these months at sea there had been no case of scurvy, but fresh food and water must be found at once if such a record of health was to be maintained. Moreover, the ship's planking must be caulked, sails repaired, barnacles and weeds scraped from the copper. A camp was soon established on shore. The casks were refilled. Woodcutters procured fuel from a land that seemed to be one entire forest. The armorer laid out in the sun the ship's stock of gunpowder to dry. While the scientists sought rare plants and birds, and some of the sailors hunted edible foods, others were set to boiling the tar that secured the ship's seams and joints below the water line. Both ship and shore hummed with activity.

It was not long before bands of New Zealand natives (or Maoris, as they called themselves) approached the Englishmen with tokens of friendship. For nails and axes they willingly exchanged eggs and fruit and sweet potatoes. Cook rejoiced in the opportunity to learn at last something about the natives of this remarkable land. In the barren regions of Poverty Bay, where living was hard, the tribes had been warlike and hostile; but here in Queen Charlotte Sound, with its abundant food, the savages were eager to be friendly. Living as they did in a stone age, the Maoris showed an ingenuity that amazed the strangers. Their forests abounded in fine timber, and it was here that Cook first saw the noble *kauri* pine. One tree, at a height of sixty feet above the ground, measured nineteen feet in circumference. It was as straight as an arrow, with little taper. Felling such trees by means of stone axes was tremendous labor. Despite this difficulty, the Maoris cut planks over sixty feet long and twelve inches wide. Their canoes and houses alike were decorated with intricate wood carvings made by means of sharpened bone and shell. Their axes were hewn from greenstone, which looked like jade but was extremely hard, and in their simple form they were of great beauty.

Except for the blue tattooing—designed to frighten enemies—the Maoris were as handsome as the Tahitians, whose language resembled their own. Born seafarers, they supplied James Cook with valuable information about the coasts and harbors. From them he learned that New Zealand was made up of two islands, and he determined at once to sail around and chart them both. At the suggestion of Joseph Banks, the passage between the North and South Islands was marked on the chart as "Cook Strait"—a name which it bears to this day. In his mind's eye Cook could see this gracious land settled by the men and women of England. The possibilities of his discovery seemed boundless.

During the months that followed, more than 2,400 miles of coast were charted, and Cook christened capes, bays, rivers and islands according to the events appropriate to them: Abundance Bay, Thirsty Bay, Oyster River, etc. The labor was a monument to his ability. But by this time he felt that the Admiralty's instructions had been fulfilled. It was time to think of home.

Two routes presented themselves: the eastward, by way of Cape Horn; and the westward, by way of the Dutch East Indies. He decided on the latter. In Java provisions could be bought for the long and taxing journey. Moreover, such a route would serve a double purpose. The island continent called Australia (around which Tasman had sailed) lay but a mere thousand miles to the west. The great Dutchman had charted only a small strip of coast without landing. Nothing was known about the country's interior. Here was a challenge not to be ignored. At least not by James Cook!

Eighteen days after dropping New Zealand astern, the first land birds of the new continent were sighted. Before James Cook turned in to sleep that night, he wrote in his journal, "I feel that I stand on the brink of a great revelation."

How true was his instinct!

It was Lieutenant Hicks, officer of the morning watch, who roused the Captain.

"It's land, sir!" the officer cried excitedly. "Two leagues off the weather bow—"

Cook sprang to his feet, fighting down the emotion that swept through him.

"A low shore, sir," Hicks rushed on, "with a rocky point to the south."

Australia . . . last of the world's great discoveries. . . . Cook controlled his voice. "Excellent, Lieutenant. When I make my chart, remind me to give a name to that point. Shall we call it 'Point Hicks'?"

The officer's youthful face flushed with pride. "Thank you, sir," he stammered. "I do thank you—"

Contrary winds and treacherous currents warned the *Endeavour* to keep her distance. To the harrassed Sailing Master there appeared to be no safe anchorage. Smoke fires could be seen through the telescope—signals, perhaps, of the aborigines. At one place a group of naked black men appeared to be following the ship along the shore. They bore no resemblance to the handsome Polynesians.

Not until the twenty-ninth day of April, 1770, was the *Endeavour* able to let her anchors go in the shelter of a splendid harbor. Because of its many fine plant specimens, the spot was immediately named "Botany Bay."

A huddle of crude shelters—not unlike those of the natives of Tierra del Fuego—could be seen on the beach. The women and children took to cover at once while half a dozen men, their black bodies streaked with white paint, came forward to challenge the Englishmen. Some of the savages were armed with spears, others with strange wooden weapons that resembled a sickle and were called boomerangs. The spears were promptly hurled, but poorly aimed and easily dodged. The marines retaliated by firing a volley above the heads of the black men, who at once took to their heels, leaving the women and children behind. Uttering strange birdlike cries, the women in turn abandoned their children and escaped into the bush. Australia lay open to the invader.

Drums rolled to a triple salvo of the guns, and men bared their heads as the Union Jack was hoisted. In the name of His Majesty King George III, the region was christened "New South Wales." The Crown of England sparkled with another jewel.

In the days to come, Cook and his men found themselves unmolested by the savages. Here was a splendid land of fertile soil. Soaring trees of fine timber were filled with birds of many varieties, while the bay itself was alive and teeming with fish. Enormous mussels and oysters were found in abundance. When Cook sat down to write in his matter-of-fact journal, he could not have guessed that he was making a remarkable prophecy about Australia:

> In this extensive country it can never be doubted but what most sorts of grain, fruits, roots, etc., of every kind would flourish were they once brought hither, planted and cultivated. And here are provender for more cattle, at all seasons of the year, than ever can be brought into the country.

Perhaps some small part of James Cook still remained a farmer's son. Yet even the fertility of New Zealand had not moved him to commit himself in such glowing terms. Australia, he felt, was a continent that would enrich England incomparably.

An occasional native, less timid than his fellows, at last made offers of friendship. Others followed suit. From them Cook gained valuable information concerning the flora and fauna. Perhaps the most astonishing discovery was that of the kangaroo—an animal that, instead of moving on all fours, leaped in vast bounds on its hind legs. Joseph Banks wrote in his own journal, "What to liken him to I cannot tell, since nothing I have ever seen resembles him." Surely this was a land of marvels!

But despite the thrill of adding a new continent to their country's glory, the crew of the *Endeavour* had had enough of voyaging. They longed for England. Below decks, in the dark of the night, whispers of mutiny could be heard —of setting the Captain and his officers adrift. Before long these rumors trickled back to the quarter-deck, disturbing the scientists and causing grave concern among the officers. But their Captain had once been a foremast hand himself. How well he understood the spirit which breeds mutiny! The sooner Cook's ship reached the Dutch East Indies the better.

But the *Endeavour's* good luck was wearing thin. She blundered into a vast trap of reefs, utterly unknown since no white man had ever been in this region. Here was the Great Barrier Reef of Australia—a labyrinth of coral extending for a thousand miles, where surf boiled over submerged rocks and treacherous currents met in a sea of conflict. Against that mighty barrier of coral, league-long breakers thundered with fury. Somehow, through this dangerous maze, James Cook must find a safe passage into the open ocean.

Sail was at once reduced to double-reefed tops'ls. Two men in the chains were casting the lead every half-hour. A dinghy was sent ahead to sound out a channel. Lookouts were posted at each masthead. Fortunately the weather was clear, the wind fair. But that fateful day was never to be forgotten by those who experienced it. The sun died in a conflagration and the moon rose full and bright, and cautiously the ship stood on, making about one knot.

In the bows the leadsmen were chanting, "By the mark twenty-two. . . . By the mark twenty-one. . . ."

"Plenty of water under us now, sir," Lieutenant Hicks suggested hopefully

Cook nodded without answering. Twenty-one fathoms was ample, but somehow his anxiety quickened. He'd not breathe easily till he was clear of this devilish region!

By now the lead was being cast every ten minutes, almost as quickly as it could be heaved and hauled aboard. Again the droning voice, "By the

Then the Endeavour *blundered into a vast trap of reefs*

mark twenty. . . . By the mark seventeen. . . ."

The words had barely left the leadsman's mouth when there came a violent crash. The *Endeavour* shuddered to her keel bolts. She quivered like a hamstrung animal. Men were flung to the deck. The mizzen topmast snapped off, hurling the lookout into the sea. James Cook sprang to help the man at the wheel. A sickening dread swept through him.

Somewhere a voice cried out, "Ah, God, we're done for!" After that no one spoke. All knew what had happened. The ship had struck and lodged on a reef. After the first violent shock the *Endeavour* lay strangely, ominously still. No rocks of coral could be seen in the dark moonlit waters, but the grinding crunch of planking sounded like a knell of doom. There was not a moment to be lost.

Quietly Cook addressed his officers. "I'll have the ship lightened at once, gentlemen. Heave overside guns, casks and all ballast."

"Aye, aye, sir!"

The order was passed and the men jumped to obey. All their months of obedience to command had prepared them for this hour. The six swivel guns were heaved into the sea. The water casks were emptied. Iron ballast was hauled up from the bilges at the very bottom of the ship and thrown overboard. Topmasts were sent down. These were lashed together and flung overside where they might be retrieved if, by any miracle, the *Endeavour* should survive. In silent desperation the men worked. But in the mind of each was a terrifying awareness of his plight. The mainland was twenty miles distant. If the ship suddenly broke apart, there would not be enough small boats to accommodate the entire crew. But those who drowned would be luckier than those cast away on a savage shore for the rest of a lifetime!

As the tide began to fall, the stricken ship listed sharply. Water was pouring into the hold. Three pumps were manned; but so exhausting was the labor that the men could work no more than ten minutes at a time before collapsing on the deck. The lightening of the ship's burden went on. James Cook was everywhere present, putting new heart into the weary, encouraging those who faltered. These same men who but a few days before had been plotting mutiny, now responded with faithful obedience. Throughout the hours of that terrible night they toiled numbly.

As dawn broke on June 11th, the *Endeavour,* relieved of some fifty tons of weight, managed to free herself of the reef, but she was still leaking dangerously. A clever plan for stopping the leak was devised. Handfuls of oakum were stitched to a square of canvas to which long ropes were attached. Then the canvas was maneuvered into place under the ship's hull, where the suction of the indrawn water held it fast. The device succeeded. Soon one pump was sufficient to keep the water in the hold at a safe level. The topmasts were retrieved and sent up. Sail was set. Half water-logged as she was, the *Endeavour* responded sluggishly to the helm as she pointed her bowsprit toward the haven of the land.

A dinghy had been sent ahead to search for a place on the coast where the ship might be beached and repaired. Such a spot was soon found. Forty-eight hours after striking the reef, the ship was hauled up on the sloping bank of a river where the receding tide would leave her high and dry. The damage she had suffered was quickly revealed. The sheathing (the external timbers that protected the hull proper) had been torn away in large areas by the pounding on the reef. A great lump of coral had pierced the oak planking, leaving a hole the size of a hogshead. Fortunately the coral had broken off and wedged itself into the wound. If at any time it had worked free, the ship would have sunk like an anchor and the fate of James Cook's enterprise would never have been revealed to the outside world.

On the banks of what was soon christened "Endeavour River," the enormous labor of refitting the ship went ahead. Tents were pitched on shore, where the blacksmith set up his forge, hammering spikes out of scraps of iron. New

timbers were felled in the forest, sawed and planed. Food supplies were beginning to run dangerously low, and parties of men were sent fishing and hunting. And always there were the furtive Australian black men, hovering like shadows in the distance, setting nerves and tempers on edge. All hands knew that if the natives should attack in force, Cook's men would be overpowered since most of the ship's guns had been thrown overboard.

Six backbreaking weeks passed before the *Endeavour* was again ready for the sea. But in the very moment of triumph, once more the ship and the lives of her men were perilously endangered. Acres of grass, five or six feet high, grew along the banks of the river. It was tinder-dry. The natives had been biding their time, waiting for a favorable wind. When that wind came, they set the grass afire. Crackling and roaring, the flames swept down upon Cook's encampment. Fortunately a high tide had already floated the *Endeavour* to safety, but most of the equipment on shore was destroyed. At incredible speed the fire raced inland toward the foothills of the mountains, until the whole world seemed to be aflame.

With a sense of profound relief all hands

looked their last on Endeavour River as the ship slipped slowly downstream. Even the problem of threading a way safely through the Great Barrier Reef seemed welcome. And this time Fortune, which had tried them so severely, smiled. Ten days of artful sailing, of taking soundings at five-minute intervals, brought the ship at last into the mile-deep waters of the blue Pacific. The realization that they were safe, at least for the time being, brought men to their knees in prayer. Others with horny fists knuckled tears from their eyes. And James Cook for the first time felt weary in the very marrow of his bones.

The way to Java lay open. But day and night one pump was kept continuously going, for heavy swells battered at the tired old ship, opening her wounds.

To the crew of the *Endeavour,* Batavia looked like a vision of paradise. Once more the men could hear the speech of their kind, eat such foods as they had dreamed of, hear news of the great world they had left so far behind. What they did not know was that Java, at that time, was one of the most deadly places on earth. Ma-

laria lurked in its clogged gutters, in its swampy
canals. Within two weeks, three-quarters of the
Endeavour's crew had fallen seriously ill. Seven
of them died. Both Joseph Banks and Dr. Solander were stricken and saved their lives by moving temporarily into the hills above the town.
Finally James Cook himself was brought down
by the dread disease. His great frame alternately
shook with chills and blazed with fever. As in
a daze he saw to it that the work of refitting
his ship went relentlessly on. The hull was
scraped, rigging was repaired, new sails were sent
aloft. Fresh stores were loaded, water casks refilled.

When the day came for sailing, however, forty
of the men were too sick for sea duty. The others, red-eyed and wasted by fever, must somehow
summon the strength to do double duty in working the ship. A course was laid for the Cape of
Good Hope, at the southern tip of Africa; but
the long haul was like a race with death. Lieutenant Hicks, first to sight Australia, was the
first victim. Barely had the waves parted to receive his canvas-wrapped body when the bosun
died. Then followed the carpenter, the corporal

of marines, three midshipmen. Not a day passed without one body or more being committed to the sea. At one time there were scarcely a dozen men able to report for duty.

It tried James Cook's soul to see his fine crew thus cut down—these men he had commanded, watched over, come to know during the endless months since leaving England. It seemed as if a blight had fallen on his great enterprise, withering the fruit of discovery, turning bitter the taste of victory. When at last Table Bay was sighted, the number of the dead had climbed to thirty-eight. Like a ghost ship the *Endeavour* crept to anchorage.

New hands were recruited in the Dutch African colony. Once again the weary voyage was resumed. Cook himself had become a gaunt shadow of the man who had bade his young wife good-bye—an eternity ago, it seemed. His uniform, faded and patched, hung loosely on his frame. His officers and men were wretched scarecrows clad in little more than rags. The blasting monotony of sea and sky came to have a nightmarish quality as the weeks of May dragged imperceptibly into June. . . . Then suddenly it was July and a *new* fever swept through the ship. This time it was a fever of anticipation. Somewhere off beyond those endless leagues of ocean, not too far, lay England.

"Land ho! *Land ho-o-o!*"

Once again the magical cry soared upward. Men crowded the bulwarks. Silent now, they stared with misted eyes at the far headlands of home. James Cook's heart leaped ahead to the house in Mile End Road, to the girl who had waited there so confidently, to the child he had never seen.

But his voice was controlled as he turned to his first officer. "Crack on all the sail she'll carry, Lieutenant," he said. "Set pennants at every masthead. This is a King's ship. We'll not come limping home!"

The voyage had lasted just sixteen days less than three years.

8 Lost Continent

Fame broke like a clap of thunder over James Cook's head. Word of his achievement spread throughout England. The Lords of the Admiralty were astounded by the extent of his charts and journals, and it did not escape their attention that he had sailed his ship with a clean bill of health as far as Java—something hitherto unheard of. Not one death from scurvy! Further-

more, along with Cook's charts—with his tales of
kangaroos and savages and pearls—the man had
brought back an empire.

Lieutenant Cook was promptly promoted to
the rank of commander. Elizabeth fairly burst
with pride for her husband. She knew he had
hoped to be made a captain; but she knew also
how rigid were the Navy's rules of seniority. In
any case, important persons now sought out this
husband of hers. Ministers received him. In a
Yorkshire village called Great Ayton, an old man
reminisced fondly of his son who had gone to
sea.

Not for long, however, would the new Commander be allowed to enjoy the peace of his
home, his wife's tender care, or the small boy
who clung like a barnacle to his famous father.
For that crotchety Scotsman, Alexander Dalrymple (chief map-maker of the Royal Navy and an
old enemy of James Cook) had examined the
newly made charts. The public acclaim of Cook's
success was a thorn in Dalrymple's side. Pomp-
ously the man stated that James Cook had not
sufficiently explored the Pacific Ocean to deny
the existence of a great southern continent. Such
a land, in Dalrymple's stubborn opinion, *did*

exist and Cook was only a clever imposter—a juggler of sights and soundings.

Presently this idea caught the public's fickle fancy. Why, everyone knew that rivers of gold flowed in the great southern continent, whose fifty million inhabitants were of a superior race! The nation who first claimed such a prize would become mistress of the world. People remem· bered suddenly that Cook was only a farmer's son and perhaps not so great a hero as they had been led to believe.

The First Lord of the Admiralty, Lord Sandwich, began to be disturbed. He was not too certain of Dalrymple's theory; but England would become the laughingstock of the world if another nation discovered and took possession of an unknown continent. Cook had not actually *proved* such a land to be non-existent. He had merely failed to find it. It was King George himself who settled the matter. Either James Cook or Alexander Dalrymple was at fault. A second expedition must be outfitted at once to clear up the matter. Cook must prove that he deserved his new commission.

Unmoved, Cook listened to these rumors. He knew that he had done his utmost. Yet the prospect of another voyage did not dismay him. Already he was growing restless among landsmen. Dearly as he loved his family, the salt sea was in his blood. In fancy he could see the palm trees of Tahiti tossing in the trade wind, New Zealand's snow-clad peaks glistening in the sun. The song of the sea still hummed within the conch shell of his childhood.

For the second expedition he insisted on two ships instead of one. Again he turned to the Whitby yards, finding two vessels that had been built in sturdy collier fashion. He christened them the *Resolution* and the *Adventure,* himself assuming command of the former. The latter was offered to an excellent naval officer named Lieutenant Furneaux. Both ships were provisioned for a voyage of two and a half years. Furneaux smiled indulgently over Cook's precautions against scurvy, saying that he'd not have *his* ship loaded down with a cargo of pickled cabbages! Months later he was to rue his folly.

Many of the men and officers who had served on the *Endeavour* begged to be allowed to sail again with the leader they so admired. This time Cook would have at his disposal 112 officers and men. His sturdy ship mounted twenty-four guns. The *Adventure* carried eighty-one men, twenty guns. Goats, sheep, pigs and crates of cackling fowl were taken aboard—those that survived would be left in due time with the natives of the South Seas. A new group of scientists had been chosen, as had a famous painter who would draw pictures of "every object which the pen of the travelers could not sufficiently describe." The Admiralty's orders read that the two ships were to enter "every corner of the South Pacific Ocean not yet examined, in order to settle once for all the existence of a southern continent."

By June 21, 1772, all was ready. James Cook bade his family good-bye. Elizabeth did her utmost to hold back the tears. Fondly the man embraced her, then held against his breast for a moment the small son he loved so deeply.

The little boy gripped the lapels of his father's fine uniform. "Someday, Dadder," he piped, pleadingly, "you take me too?"

"Someday, son, for sure," the man promised, meaning every word. "But you've got to grow big and strong to fist a sail. Meanwhile, watch over your mother till I come home."

On the heels of a fair wind the two ships laid a course for the Cape of Good Hope. There, three and a half months later, the governor of the Dutch colony informed the Englishmen that a French ship had recently touched that port, with the objective of searching for the great southern continent. The race was on!

As the ships plowed ever southward, the cold became intense. Officers and crew alike were outfitted with woolen clothing, topped off by a short jacket known as a "fearnaught." But it was impossible to keep warm or dry. The galley stove was the only source of heat in either ship and a man could rely for comfort only on the warmth within his own body. Much of the livestock, huddled in pens on the fo'c'slehead, perished of exposure to the icy wind. Rain turned to sleet, then to blinding, driving snow. Sails froze like sheets of metal, against which the crew hammered with bloody fists.

As the ships approached the Antarctic Circle, icebergs appeared out of fog and snow, sometimes terrifyingly close at hand. One such was judged to be a hundred feet high, its walls like a mighty cliff against which waves dashed in fury. The iceberg was so close that the ship was

Porpoises frolicked about the two lonely ships

unable to come about and gain steerageway. The only chance was to haul as close to the wind as possible. There were seconds of agonizing suspense while the *Resolution* cleared the iceberg with barely fifty feet to spare.

The ice was covered with birds that looked like little men in black and white suits: the first penguins anyone had ever seen. Great whales frolicked about the ship, while albatrosses swept low, muttering their mournful cries. It was a scene inexpressibly wild and dreary, plunging all hands into despair. These same men who had begged the privilege of sailing with the great Captain Cook now bewailed their lot. Genius or madman—which was this Cook? As for Cook himself, he remained locked within the loneliness of command. He would never turn back until, once and for all, he had disposed of the myth of the Great Southern Continent.

Lack of drinking water now became serious. Fortunately it was discovered that sea ice, when melted, became fresh and sweet. Cook ordered out the boats and soon had fifteen tons of ice on board. On Christmas Day the lookout at the masthead counted more than a hundred ice islands, some of which were half a mile long and none smaller than the ship. The crew had saved their ration of grog for this day, but it was a sorry celebration.

On January 17, 1773, the Antarctic Circle was crossed for the first time in history. Here a storm of great violence raged, during which the two ships became separated. For three days Cook cruised back and forth among the ice floes, searching for his consort. Flares were lighted at night. Guns were fired at regular intervals by day. But the *Adventure* had disappeared as completely as if the ocean had parted to swallow her alive, which, indeed, many believed to be the case. The Captain of the *Resolution* took what comfort he could from the fact that he had foreseen just such an emergency. It had been arranged that if the two ships parted they would meet in Queen Charlotte Sound in New Zealand.

With the disappearance of the *Adventure*, spirits aboard the *Resolution* plunged even deeper in despair. With another vessel for company, the men had not known such utter dejection as they now felt. Eastward and westward to infinity the great ice pack extended. Time and again the ship narrowly escaped destruction. Nor did it improve matters to realize that this season was the Antarctic summer. What would the winter be like? Anxiously men and officers eyed their Captain, but none dared broach the matter uppermost in the thoughts of all: when would they turn back? But James Cook was not a man to be turned back easily. Despite gales and wild seas, for another month the *Resolution* held her easterly course in a latitude of 60° S.

During the night of February 17th the sky was illuminated by vast bands of mysterious light —spirals of color that bathed sea and ice in eerie glow. Here was the aurora australis, counterpart of the aurora borealis of the north. But the superstitious sailors saw in it only a confirmation of their doom.

In latitude 67° 15', it became evident that no way could be found through the limitless ice fields. No ship before had ever sailed so far south. Surely Dalrymple's theory of a lost continent had been exploded. James Cook gave at last the long awaited order to turn north, and the men sprang to obey. They had been at sea for 117 days on end. They had sailed 3,500 miles of ocean without once sighting land.

New Zealand hove on the horizon as fair and radiant as a dream. In Queen Charlotte Sound the *Adventure* rode safely at anchor. But two of her men had died of scurvy and fifteen others were seriously ill. These latter were just beginning to mend on a diet of fruits and vegetables. Lieutenant Furneaux, who privately had scoffed at Cook as a food crank, revised his opinion.

The livestock that had survived the Antarctic were set ashore: a few sheep and a number of pigs. If at some future day Englishmen decided to found a colony in this far land, they would find familiar creatures waiting for them. Carrots were planted, turnips, potatoes and parsnips too, and the friendly Maoris of the region were instructed in the care of them.

In holiday mood the two ships sailed north, touching briefly at Tahiti for wood and water. Old King Tutaha and his consort made much of the officers, while the natives embraced the crew even as they stole from them.

West of Tahiti, a chain of more than a hundred islands was discovered. They were peopled by a race so friendly and handsome that Cook at once christened the group the "Friendly Islands." Then sailing in a wide circle through the

Pacific, the ships touched at the Marquesas Islands, whose exact position had never been fixed on any map. Then they went south again to Easter Island, where colossal stone statues lined the shore, mocking all efforts to pierce the mystery of their origin. Here the country was poor, the water bad, and the few inhabitants—living in the shadow of the strange black statues—had little to offer in the way of food.

Up anchor and off again! Wherever he sailed, James Cook enriched the existing charts of the Pacific with new discoveries, among which were Norfolk Island and New Caledonia. The latter he found to be the largest in this part of the Pacific. Scores of lesser islands were discovered, christened, and their positions fixed for all time.

But Dalrymple's lost continent haunted James Cook like a specter. He would not turn back from his search without one last effort in the icy waters south of New Zealand. Thus it happened that for weeks to come the two ships rolled and plunged in the stormy seas that stretched halfway to the coast of South America. Here the *Adventure* once more disappeared. Again all signals went unanswered. Had she foundered in the mighty gales of the prevailing westerlies known by sailors as the "roaring forties"? That question would go unanswered for many months.

Then the incredible happened. James Cook fell ill. He was now in his forty-sixth year, and many of those years had been spent in as hard a life as a man could know. His gaunt frame was like the oaken timbers of a ship which had been battered too long by wind and wave. He was able to sleep only in snatches. He could retain neither food nor medicine. He came as close to dying as a man may come and still live. Mr. Patten, the ship's surgeon, despaired of saving his life. To the crew and officers of the *Resolution* it was unbelievable that their commander—the man they had obeyed, cursed, loved—should die. Silent as ghosts they went about the business of working ship. It was a day for rejoicing when Patten at last brought the word aloft, "He is better today, God bless him!"

The Admiralty's instructions had been fulfilled. No ship had ever sailed farther or more perilously. Now it was time to think of home. James Cook's recovery was rapid. He determined to sail by the Cape Horn route, which was still imperfectly charted. He would correct that! Despite foul weather and the burning impatience of his men, he surveyed the entire region before beginning the long homeward haul across the Atlantic.

And when at last the lookout sighted the hills of Plymouth, the *Resolution* had been gone for three years and sixteen days. She had explored 20,000 leagues of sea, losing only four men. Not one had died of scurvy. The *Adventure*, badly battered, had reached home port a year earlier.

The final entry in James Cook's journal read: "I have made the circuit of the Southern Ocean in a high latitude, and traversed it in such manner as to leave not the least room for the possibility of there being a continent, unless near the Pole, and so out of reach of navigation."

So much for Alexander Dalrymple!

Once more James Cook enjoyed the quiet peace of his family. But one day a messenger appeared in Mile End Road, bearing a roll of parchment officially sealed. It was James Cook's commission as a captain in the Royal Navy. The parchment bore the seal and signature of His Majesty King George III. Furthermore, Captain Cook was summoned to an early audience with the King at St. James's Palace.

For a moment Cook could hardly believe the overwhelming fact. Elizabeth stood by his side, not speaking. She glanced up at the tall, lean Yorkshireman with the fine forehead and bold nose, the cheek burned to mahogany by the suns and winds of the seven seas—this man who was her husband. And perhaps, being a wise woman, she guessed something of what was passing in his mind.

He was remembering the fields of Great Ayton, where he had toiled at his father's side . . . the boy in homespun breeches on the morning he had left the valley of his birth, his mother clinging to him to whisper, "God keep you, son, and bring you home" . . . the long and lonely years. . . . All had been planned to this end. He, James Cook, a farmer's son, was now a captain in the Royal Navy.

"Do I really deserve this honor of His Majesty?" he asked of the woman who clung to his hand.

Swift and sure came Elizabeth's answer. "Deserve it? No other man has ever done more for England. You were born a captain!"

He turned to look down at her, and his eyes—so true a blue—kindled. The twist of his lips was tender. "A good sailor makes a poor husband, Elizabeth."

"Not *my* sailor," she answered, and drew his head down to hers.

9 The Farthest Shore

Alexander Dalrymple retreated into stubborn silence. *His* day was over. For this time James Cook had returned as a hero whose name and achievements were on every tongue. Spain, Holland, France and Russia—all acknowledged the exploits of the greatest navigator the world had known.

The Royal Society—that fearsome body!—

unanimously elected Cook to membership. The former Whitby shipyard apprentice himself read the paper he had written on the methods used to protect the health of his crew during a three-year voyage. At the end of the year this paper won for its writer the Sir Godfrey Copley gold medal: England's highest honor for experimental work.

When the president of the Royal Society called the name of Captain Cook, to present the medal, the applause was thunderous. But it was a woman, still slim and young, who rose to acknowledge the acclaim. Elizabeth Cook had come alone to accept the honor in her husband's behalf. He himself had already departed to explore new worlds.

Cook's third and last voyage came about in this fashion: For two centuries navigators had been seeking a shorter route to link the Atlantic Ocean with the Pacific. If such a passage could be discovered on the northwest coast of America, England's commerce with the Far East would be greatly speeded.

King George offered a reward of 20,000 pounds to any British navigator who discovered such a short cut. The idea was not new. Sir

Francis Drake, Henry Hudson, Jacques Cartier —all had been fired by the possibility of a Northwest Passage. The very thought of it was tinder for the fuse of such a soaring mind as James Cook's.

It was the First Lord of the Admiralty who proposed that a fresh attempt should be made in North American waters. Only one man occurred to Lord Sandwich as the possible leader of such an expedition: Captain James Cook. But His Lordship hesitated to suggest this proposal to a man recently returned from a long and perilous voyage. Cook should be allowed to enjoy his family in peace. Nevertheless, Lord Sandwich invited the famous navigator to dinner one evening with Sir Hugh Palliser. Here were three old and tried friends together.

When finally the conversation worked around to the Northwest Passage, the First Lord turned to James Cook and said, "You, my good friend, can give me better advice in this matter than anyone else. Whom do you suggest that I place at the head of such an expedition?"

Without a moment's hesitation came Cook's reply. "Myself, Your Lordship."

Sir Hugh and his host exchanged smiles. England need not fear for her glory! Her finest sailor was about to take the helm once more.

On February 10, 1776, Cook's appointment was ratified by the King.

As gently as he could, the great navigator broke the news to his beloved wife. Once again Elizabeth accepted the announcement bravely. As any other woman, she had often dreamed of a quiet home where she and her husband, side by side, might watch two fine sons grow to manhood. The long years of waiting, of anxiety, had left their mark in the fine lines about Elizabeth's mouth, in the drift of white that touched her dark hair. But her eyes were still as young as those of the girl who had faced this same man a lifetime ago in the shabby lodgings in Shadwell —the girl who had said, "Oh, to be able to do such things! How dull the rest of us must seem to you. . . ."

Now Elizabeth, the woman, turned to her husband and laid a hand on his arm. Her voice was low and clear. "Men like you, my dearest one, never belong to their wives and children. They belong to the world—to history. But, oh! Promise me one thing, just *one*—"

"And that, my Elizabeth?"

"That when you come home from *this* voyage, you will never leave us again."

James Cook took his wife in his arms. He looked down into her troubled eyes. "I promise," he vowed, solemnly. "The years to come belong to you. Exploration is for younger men than I. When I come home, I shall swallow the anchor and stay ashore forevermore."

Elizabeth smiled up at him. "Just to remind you of your promise, I shall place a lighted lamp in the window every night until you return."

"A beacon, eh?" The man humored her. "I have followed one all my life!"

Two vessels—the *Resolution* and the *Discovery* —were chosen for the Northwest expedition. The former already had proved her mettle and the latter had been built in the same Whitby yards. Captain Clerke, a splendid officer and one of Cook's lieutenants on a former voyage, was appointed to command of the *Discovery*.

Many of the officers and men who had been part of the first and second expeditions begged to join the third one. Here was proof, if proof were needed, of the true worth of this leader of men. Lord Sandwich saw that the Admiralty spared no expense in outfitting the two ships. Since all previous circumnavigators of the world had returned to Europe by way of the Cape of Good Hope, Cook's instructions were to return to England by the high northern latitudes between America and Asia, entering the Atlantic Ocean from the Pacific by means of the Northwest Passage which most men still believed must exist.

On July 12, 1776—amid a flutter of bunting and wildly cheering crowds—the *Resolution* and the *Discovery* cleared Plymouth Harbor. Braced on the quarter-deck, James Cook watched the coast of England fade and disappear. In spite of the fine ship he commanded, the splendid crew and the voyage that stretched ahead with a promise of glory, his heart lay heavy in his breast. Perhaps destiny, hovering above a man's head, sometimes sweeps close enough for him to feel the brush of its wing. Cook's thoughts flew to his wife and sons, to his old father drowsing by the fire in Great Ayton. When would he see them again and hear their voices?

Reaching the Cape of Good Hope in December, the two ships re-provisioned for the long

voyage into upper Pacific waters. Here were familiar latitudes and Cook touched at islands he
had known before. He was in no hurry. If a
Northwest Passage existed, it would always be
there.

For a full year he cruised among the islands,
adding a vast store of material to the scientific
knowledge of the world and cementing friendship between the English and the Polynesians. At
the Friendly Islands the two ships were given
a royal welcome. And at every island that he
touched, Cook left livestock, plants, seeds and
whatever metal could be spared.

Then, sailing north, on Christmas Eve the
great navigator discovered an atoll which proved
to be one of the largest lagoon islands in the
world. Advantage was taken of an eclipse of the
sun to establish the longtitude of this island and
set the ships' watches.

The land itself was incredibly barren, devoid
of palms and without drinking water. But its
forty-mile lagoon teemed with every form of marine life that swam, crawled or slithered. The
shores were covered with countless millions of
nesting sea birds so unaccustomed to the sight of
man that they showed not the slightest fear. The

sailors killed great numbers of seals, whose fat was highly prized. A cairn of stones was discovered, to which a bottle had been fastened by a piece of wire. A strip of parchment within the bottle stated that a French ship had anchored in the harbor four years previously. On the back of the parchment Cook inscribed a record of his own visit: "Ships *Resolution* and *Discovery,* of his Britannic Majesty. December 1777." He replaced the parchment and sealed the bottle with lead. Then, building the cairn higher so that it might be seen from the bay, he ordered the Union Jack hoisted. Thus Christmas Island stepped into history.

Northward through the Pacific the two ships beat their way. Now James Cook was entering regions unknown to him. He came upon a group of eight splendid islands, more fertile than any he had yet seen, and at once christened them the "Sandwich Islands," in honor of the First Lord of the Admiralty. (Later this discovery would be known as the Hawaiian Islands.) Knowing that he must take advantage of the summer weather on the North American coast, Cook lingered at his new discovery only long enough to ship wood and water. But he promised himself a longer visit on his return, for he was convinced that the Sandwich Islands were the most important discovery he had yet made in the Pacific.

By March of 1778, the Northwest Coast was sighted. The two ships dropped anchor in a bay that Cook named "King George's Bay," now known as Nootka Sound. The tide was at flood and reached far up the beach, joining together sea and land. The air was mountain cold and of great purity. There was a sound of waterfalls, of strange bird cries, and a pungent smell of evergreen smoke. The crew was intrigued by this savage land, so different from the balmy isles of the South Seas. Men and officers alike lined the bulwarks. (Among Cook's officers was a young man named George Vancouver, destined to play an important part in the history of that coast.)

Fleets of canoes, filled with Indians, shot out from the beach. It could be seen that the squaws were at the paddles—an indication of good will. The men alone came aboard the ships, with their bundles of furs for trade. Agilely they scrambled up the chains, ropes, ladders—by any finger hold they could grip. They came like a swarm of locusts descending on a fertile valley. The air shrilled with their high, falsetto clamor. They were incredibly dirty, their hair was matted and greased, their bodies were streaked with painted symbols. Lean and rangy, they moved with a sort of reckless arrogance. They roved about the ship like inquisitive monkeys, prying into every object that caught their fancy. Only the fact that they were unarmed reassured the ship's company.

For trade the savages offered the pelts of wolves, bears, martens and sea otters. They would accept nothing in exchange except copper. It seemed that from the traders who had already penetrated their forests, they had acquired a familiarity with metal. Soon both ships were stripped of copper, even to the buttons on the sailors' jackets. The Indians proved to be even cleverer thieves than the natives of the South Seas. Not so much as a fishhook or a bent nail escaped their covetous eyes. Their own possessions, however, they guarded jealously, exacting high payment from the Englishmen for water, food and even grass for the livestock. Quick to take offense, they were quicker still to avenge the smallest slight. Cook's men were forced to be on constant guard.

At length the two ships cruised north. The

months that followed were employed in surveying the coast. Charts were made, soundings taken, capes and bays named as James Cook sought in vain for the elusive Northwest Passage. Again and again he encountered new tribes of Indians, fierce and treacherous, many of whom traded their furs with the Russians in the north.

Sailing finally through Bering Strait, the *Resolution* and the *Discovery* navigated the frozen waters of the Arctic Ocean. Before turning south again, Cook had touched the shores of Asia and America surrounding the strait. With the approach of summer's end, he deemed it inadvisable to tarry longer in these frozen regions. He resolved to pass the winter in the Sandwich Islands, where his men could recuperate and he would have an opportunity to chart the islands more fully.

On his way south, however, he threaded his way through a difficult passage called Unalaska. There, while both ships were being overhauled, he and Captain Clerke each received a curious present. It was delivered by a native, and proved to be a pie made of rye meal filled with highly seasoned salmon. A letter, which no one could read, accompanied the gift.

"The Indians have no written language that ever I knew," Clerke observed. "What do you make of it, sir?"

"It must be Russian," the other surmised. " 'Tis said they trade all through this region."

Cook instructed a young marine corporal, John Ledyard (who later carved an adventurous career of his own), to search for the mysterious donor. Several days later Ledyard returned accompanied by three Russians—the first Europeans the Englishmen had seen for two years. In spite of language difficulties, it was learned that the strangers were engaged in fur trade to the north. One of the men, named Ismyloff, showed Cook a map he had made of the Kurile Islands, the Kamchatka Peninsula and all the discoveries to the east that had been made by the Russians.

Toasts were drunk, a sumptuous meal was consumed. When the visitors took their leave, Cook entrusted to Ismyloff a letter for the British Admiralty. With the letter Cook enclosed a map of all the northern shores he himself had visited. The Russian hoped, in the spring, to find means of sending out the letter. He made good his promise. One year later, passed from hand to hand across Siberia, Cook's precious news reached London.

Leaving northern latitudes behind, the two ships laid a course for the Sandwich Islands. Days later (November 30, 1778) the largest island of the group, known as Hawaii, rose on the horizon. To sun-starved men, the island was as beautiful as a dream. Green, fertile slopes rose tier upon tier to summits that glistened with everlasting snow. Of all the islands of the Pacific, Hawaii was the fairest.

Contrary winds held the ships offshore, warning them away. As the *Resolution* tacked doggedly around Hawaii's southernmost cape, trailed by her consort, fleets of canoes put out to sea. These frail craft were laden to the gunwales with gifts of food—pigs, fruit, sugar cane. The smiling natives, flower-decked, seemed to be amphibious—swimming great distances without the least appearance of fatigue.

Ahead lay a wide bay half encircled by volcanic cliffs. The master's mate, one William Bligh, was sent ashore to reconnoitre for anchorage. (This was the same Bligh who later would become notorious as master of the *Bounty*.) In this case Bligh did his work well. The ships were brought to anchor opposite a beach of volcanic ash, where a stream of fresh water emptied into the sea. On shore, magnificent palm trees dozed above their own shadows, sheltering thatched houses from the sun's glare.

Now hundreds of canoes, filled with joyous men and women, swarmed around the ships. Bronze-skinned children clambered up the chains and rigging and tumbled on the decks like playful puppies. How different from the surly Indians of the Northwest Coast! Here were only smiles, gifts, songs and happy greetings. Few among the Englishmen were sorry that a Northwest Passage for home had not been discovered! But they had difficulty in pronouncing the name of this extraordinary place: Kealakekua.

With great ceremony King Kalaniopuu and his priests announced their arrival. Helmets made from thousands of tiny feathers crowned their heads. Magnificent cloaks of red and yellow plumes—the hallmark of royalty—swept from their shoulders to the deck. These Hawaiians were handsome men, above the average height and not unlike the Tahitians whose language resembled their own.

Koa, the High Priest and King's Prime Minister, stepped forward to address James Cook. For intuitively, it seemed, these primitive people had singled out the supreme leader among the Englishmen. In the native tongue Koa made a long speech, not one word of which James Cook could understand. Unfortunately that speech (could Cook have guessed it) had much to do with the disastrous events which later occurred.

This is what Koa was saying: "In remote times, O White Man, there lived in this island a god named Lono. In a fit of rage Lono slew his wife and children. Overcome with remorse at what he had done, he fled Hawaii and ascended into the sky. From there he called down to his followers, 'Someday I shall return, O my people, in a great canoe with white wings. And all shall be the same between us as before.' "

Here Koa, the High Priest, paused for a moment before bringing his speech of welcome to a close. "Your canoe is mighty and it has great wings, O White Man," he concluded. "You have returned to us. *You* are Lono!" Here the old Hawaiian knelt and struck his forehead three times against the deck, while King Kalaniopuu and his followers paid similar homage to the English Captain. Even the playful children fell silent, bowing their dark heads in imitation of their elders.

Cook and his officers were nonplussed. Of old Koa's harangue they had caught only the word *Lono*.

Completely mystified, Captain Clerke muttered to his superior, "What in the name of St. James was the old fellow talking about?"

"I am at sea," the other answered, bewildered and embarrassed. "They are behaving as if we were gods."

"A difficult role to sustain," came Clerke's dry answer, "even for an Englishman. I trust that our crew will not disillusion them. What do you suppose *Lono* means?"

James Cook could not recall having heard the word among Polynesians.

At that moment, ceremoniously, the High Priest flung over the Captain's shoulders one of the splendid feather robes—the Hawaiian mark of greatest reverence. Only the highest born might wear the feather cloaks. To the Sandwich Islanders the mighty white-winged canoe and its

Master were the realization of the legend of Lono. These strangers were not mortals. They were gods who would live forever. They could not die. They could do no wrong.

After the ceremony Cook solemnly accompanied King Kalaniopuu ashore. There he was conducted to the *heiau,* or sacred place. This was a lofty stone altar built for the observance of all religious rites. On the platform of the *heiau* the King and the British Captain exchanged names —the sacred token of friendship among Pacific islanders. While the priests kept up a tireless chant, Kalaniopuu placed his own feather helmet on the Englishman's head. Cook offered his gold-braided cocked hat in exchange, and girded about the King's waist his own belt and sword. Now the welcome to Lono was complete and absolute. All unknowing, James Cook had assumed the mantle of divinity. Gifts poured aboard the ships: pigs, fruits, coconuts, bananas, bolts of native cloth made from the inner bark of the mulberry tree. The decks were heaped high. Nothing was demanded in return. No one knew what to make of such lavish hospitality. In no other part of the Pacific had its like been seen.

But James Cook was impatient to get on with

surveying the island shores. Native ceremonies at length exasperated him. He had no wish to be treated as a god. The next day arrangements were made to erect on shore an observatory for the nautical instruments. Koa, the High Priest, chose a suitable place and pronounced it *taboo,* or sacred. The ships eased in to closer anchorage in order to cover the encampment with their guns. In spite of the whole-hearted welcome, in Cook's opinion it was folly to be caught unguarded.

The weeks were slipping rapidly away, and the year 1778 came to a close with less accomplished than the great navigator would have wished.

Suddenly an unfortunate incident occurred. A gunner's mate died. His body was carried ashore for burial. The Hawaiians were thrown into consternation. How could this immortal, this servant of the great god Lono, *die?*

Uncertainty rumbled like far-off thunder through the ranks of the Hawaiians. The mighty ship with white sails—was it really the winged canoe in which Lono had promised to return? And the Great White Chief himself—was he an impostor? Doubt spread like wildfire, fanned by the wind of suspicion. King Kalaniopuu told his people that they had been deceived. The white strangers had accepted their gifts falsely. They were not gods. They were mortals who could die, even as the man who had just been buried in their own earth. . . .

Thus the feeling grew, day by day. Gifts no longer poured aboard the ships. Sailors, refilling the water casks on shore, were greeted by showers of stones. Petty thievery began. The most able native swimmers came in the night to extract the very nails from the ships' planking. Cook's protests were of no avail. It seemed as if the King himself encouraged the thieves.

As leader of the expedition, James Cook felt this to be a personal defeat. From the very beginning of his voyages he had shown a natural understanding of primitive peoples. Like children they flocked to him with instinctive trust. Of them all he most admired the Hawaiians. And now a sense of failure settled upon him, clouding his judgment. For the moment he forgot that no man had ever journeyed farther than he over the earth's surface, nor left more indelibly a splendid record. True, he had not found the

Northwest Passage. But he had discovered these fertile islands, finest in the Pacific, only to earn the mistrust of their inhabitants. Suddenly, in his hour of defeat, he longed fiercely, achingly, to see once more the green hills of home . . . and Elizabeth.

From amidships drifted the Scottish voice of the bosun, saying, "A bonny land, this Hawaii, but it's nae Scotland. Till now I've liked it fine. But I weary for the heather and the deer."

"Aye," another voice agreed. " 'Tis nae Scotland."

"Sometimes," the bosun mused, "I wonder if I'll see the gorse again, and hear the pipes settin' my blood a-tingle wi' 'Loch Lomond,' or know the hayfields in the month o' June. . . ."

The voices found an echo in James Cook's heart.

His cup of bitterness filled when King Kalaniopuu sent a messenger aboard to find out when the strangers planned to leave. The great quantities of food showered upon the white men could mean famine to the Hawaiians.

Swiftly Cook made up his mind. The time had come to go. Word was passed through the ships. The observatory was dismantled. Silent, sullen

natives watched the preparations for departure.
There were no protests of sorrow, no farewells.
It was as if the Hawaiians were watching a pesti-
lence run its course.

By February 4th all was ready. Anchors were
weighed, all sail was set. The shores were lined
with thousands of watchful natives. To the great
relief of all hands aboard the *Resolution* and the
Discovery, the lava cliffs of Kealakekua fell rapidly away.

Then the unforeseen happened. The ships
were caught and battered by a tropical storm of
extreme violence. The *Resolution's* foremast
snapped off. The voyage could not be continued
until a new mast was raised. The nearest place
for repairs was Kealakekua.

The returning ships were greeted with open
hostility. An officer, going ashore in search of
suitable timber, was hailed by a shower of abuse.
His men were attacked by rocks and spears, and
with difficulty regained the ship alive. Worse
was to follow. That night furtive lights were
seen on shore. By dawn it was found that the
Discovery's cutter had been stolen, so stealthily
that none of the sentries had heard a sound.

Here was warfare, open and declared. But the

silent black cliffs of Kealakekua loomed above a village that seemed to be deserted. An expectant hush hung over both ships. The crews moved about their chores as if they feared to disturb the silence, as if a heavy footfall or a loud voice would be an intrusion and startling. The unbearable feeling of waiting for a blow to fall increased degree by degree until, far off in the volcanic hills, drums began to beat. Softly at first. Then louder . . . louder . . . The jungle was speaking. The earth answered. The sky held its breath.

James Cook resolved at all costs to recover the cutter, the best of his small boats. Stern measures must be taken. He determined to go ashore and confront the King himself. If necessary, he would hold Kalaniopuu as hostage for the cutter's return. Before leaving the *Resolution,* he gave orders that all canoes attempting to escape from the bay be stopped.

Accompanied by nine marines under Lieutenant Phillips, Cook took his place in the stern-sheets of the pinnace. In the crook of one arm he held a double-barreled gun. Here, he thought bitterly, was the full measure of his defeat: that

James Cook called to the native to put down his spear

he must face with gun in hand these people he
so admired.

As the boat headed in toward shore, it could
be seen that thousands of natives were gathering.
Many were armed with spears, others with *pa-
huas*—the heavy stone war clubs. Most of the warriors were protected by the wicker armor of
fighters. For so great a mass of people they were
strangely, ominously silent. King Kalaniopuu
strode through the crowd to the edge of the
beach, where he stood braced defiantly.

As the pinnace pulled into the surf a dozen
yards from shore, a volley of shots could be
heard. The boats patrolling the bay had fired
on canoes attempting to escape. A rumble of
anger surged through the crowd. The King fled,
whether from fear or caution there was no telling.

Cook sprang into the shallows. The sailors
backed water, rested on their oars. Phillips clung
to the tiller. One Hawaiian, bolder than his fellows, strode forward to confront the Captain.
Coolly, Cook called to the native to throw down
his spear. But the man's arm swept back with full
intent to kill. Cook raised the gun and fired. The
ball failed to penetrate the protective armor of

matting. Unharmed by the shot, the Hawaiian shouted defiantly and again drew back his spear. Cook fired the second barrel, killing his attacker instantly.

Pandemonium broke loose. The crowd surged forward, shouting, screeching. Spears hummed through the air. The marines fired a volley of musketry. The warriors plunged into the sea, dragging four sailors from the pinnace while others fought them off with the oars. Phillips was struck between the shoulders by a *pahua,* but with the butt end of a musket knocked his assailant down. The remaining marines fired a second ragged volley. The bullets might as well have been pebbles.

Meanwhile, James Cook had reached the edge of the shore. Alone he faced three thousand raging savages. Something of his old glory, his *taboo,* still clung to him. For the Hawaiians hesitated to attack this chief who faced them with his fearless glance. Another volley of shot rattled through the crowd, wounding a dozen warriors. Half turning, Cook shouted to Phillips to hold fire.

This generous action proved fatal. A warrior, creeping up from behind, flung himself upon the

Captain. The *pahua* thudded as it struck home. James Cook staggered, flung up his arms. He plunged face-downward into the water. Again the *pahua* descended, again and again.

The great Captain Cook—the boy who had dreamed of the sea—lay where he had fallen. Waves broke over his lifeless body.

Ten miles offshore two ships lay hove to. With stark yards and spars they wore an aspect of desolation. Flags drooped at half-mast. The ships rose and fell to the long, dreary processionals of the sea. Four bells struck as the fo'c'sle hands gathered at the *Resolution's* bulwarks. All stood with lowered heads. Hats and caps were clutched in white-knuckled hands. The sky was lowering and rain-streaked. The cliffs of Hawaii loomed dark against the sea. A gust of wind whipped at Captain Clerke's shirt; rain glistened on his cheek.

The door of the companionway opened and four sailors emerged. Between them they bore a canvas-wrapped bundle bound with hemp and draped with a faded Union Jack. On slow feet the men advanced toward the rail. Captain Clerke opened a Bible. Above the droning of the wind his hoarse voice intoned, "In my Father's house are many mansions: if it were not so I would have told you. . . ."

The fo'c'sle hands huddled closer, as if to seek warmth and reassurance from their kind. Some of the men tried to hide their emotion. Others stood with heads uplifted as tears, manly and unashamed, slid down the furrows of their cheeks. The four sailors, with no heart for their special task, balanced the canvas burden on the bulwark. The Union Jack was drawn aside.

Captain Clerke's voice seemed to push against some obstacle in his throat. . . . "We therefore commit this body to the Deep, to be turned into corruption, looking for the resurrection of the body, when the sea shall give up her dead, and the life of the world to come . . ." The voice cracked as it cried, "God's blessing on you, James Cook, and good-bye!"

More than a year passed before the news reached England. The nation was stunned by a sense of loss. It was said that the King could hardly restrain his tears as he directed that a pension of 200 pounds be awarded to the great navigator's family. The whole world acknowledged that James Cook had enriched navigation by charts of incomparable accuracy. His contributions to astronomy and natural science were beyond measure. Always a leader, he had been as exacting of himself as of others. One of England's truly great men was gone.

And every night at dusk, for many years to come, in the window of a small brick house in Mile End Road passers-by could see a light, like a beacon, burning steadfastly until dawn.

Index